Christians or Capitalists?

Christians or Capitalists?

Christianity and Politics in South Africa

Cosmas Desmond

The Bowerdean Press 1978

261.1X
D465
79062512

First published in 1978 by
The Bowerdean Press
15 Blackfriars Lane
London EC4V 6ER

Copyright © 1978 C. Desmond

Designed by Douglas Martin

Printed and Bound by
Unwin Brothers Ltd
Woking, Surrey

British Library Cataloguing in Publication Data:
Desmond, Cosmas
    Christians or capitalists?
    1. Church and social problems — South Africa
    2. Church and race relations — South Africa
    I. Title
    261.1'0968   HN801.A8

    ISBN 0-906097-03-7
    ISBN 0-906097-04-5   Pbk

Contents

Acknowledgements

This book would have taken a very different form had it not been for the influence of the South American theologians Gustavo Gutierrez, J. Miguez Bonino, H. Assman, R. Alves, J.P. Miranda, and J.L. Segundo. My indebtedness to most of them is evident from the frequency with which they are quoted in the text.

I owe a much longer-standing debt of gratitude to the work of Professor Edward Schillebeeckx. When I had completed my studies at the seminary I was advised by an older and wiser priest, the late Vincent Rochford, to forget all that I had been taught and to start reading some theology. I am grateful to him for that advice and to Schillebeeckx, more than to any other single theologian, for enabling me to follow it.

The journal *New Blackfriars* has also been a source of constant inspiration. On a more personal level, I am extremely grateful to Albert Nolan for his help and encouragement during the course of writing this book and, more particularly, for the great assistance he gave with the final editing.

My thanks are also due to Professor Colin Gardner, who, despite his many commitments, found time to read a large part of the manuscript and to offer some valuable suggestions; to Hilda Colenbrander for her expert typing; to Joan Kerchhoff, who, in addition to helping with some typing, was always a ready listener and a responsive 'sounding-board'; last but not least, to my wife for her help not only with typing but also in coping with life in general and the writing of this book in particular.

Introduction: Preaching the Gospel?

This book is addressed primarily to those White Christians who are aware of the injustice and suffering inflicted upon people by the present politico-economic system in South Africa and who acknowledge that they are obliged as Christians to be actively involved in overcoming this injustice or suffering. A commitment to bringing about a reordering of our society, not simply an intellectual conviction that change is necessary, is presupposed. I do not believe that it is possible simply to argue people into such a commitment. This can only arise as the result of experience - the experience of the evilness of the system and of the inadequacy of our present efforts to change it.

However, while knowledge alone does not produce commitment, neither does commitment alone produce the knowledge that is necessary for putting that commitment into practice. A commitment that is not questioned and reflected upon is bound to lead either to frustration or to the masochistic enjoyment of bashing one's head against a brick wall. One feels more and more strongly about the need to do something but lacks the means of giving expression to these feelings. On the other hand, knowledge about, and 'objective' analysis of, the problems we face are in themselves sterile. In South Africa, as elsewhere, there are plenty of armchair revolutionaries, whose erudition is in inverse proportion to their active political involvement. This, of course, is not meant to imply that all committed Christians are stupid or that all intellectuals are politically uncommitted.

What many White Christians in South Africa today are looking for is a 'Practical Handbook on Christian Change'. I am not, however, making any attempt to provide this, because I do not think that it is possible to do so. This impossibility arises, I believe, not simply from my own personal lack of knowledge, but from the nature of the Christian message. While the desire for clear guidelines to action is understandable, this desire arises from a particular understanding of the Christian message and of the task of theology. It is my contention that it is this understanding of the Bible and of theology, rather than any ill-will, lack of courage, or any other moral fault, that prevents White Christians from being involved in effective political activity. Any Christian's understanding of the Bible, particularly of the New Testament, must acknowledge that loving one's neighbour is central to the Christian message and essential to Christian practice. This belief alone can and does motivate people to do all sorts of good, even heroic, work for others. It has led Christians in South Africa to do much to alleviate the suffering of people - by providing material aid, medical services, education etc - and to condemn the present political system. It cannot, however, lead them any further. The conviction that we *must* love our neighbour does not tell us *how* we must do it. The more aware these Christians become of the injustice of the system and the more their moral condemnations and exhortations appear to fall on deaf ears, the more vehement they become in their denunciation. They behave rather like the Englishman abroad who believes that if you speak English slowly enough and, particularly, loudly enough anybody will understand. But many don't. Why? Because they speak a different language.

The Church's usual response to this lack of understanding is to look for more and more effective ways of communicating its message and of encouraging people to apply it in practice. This approach, however, assumes that everybody is speaking the same language: the language of the Gospel about loving one's neighbour. But in fact we can only express our understanding of the Gospel in a language that is influenced by many other factors, including social, political, and cultural ones. We cannot, therefore, give a theological or 'Christian' answer to political and social problems. How to love one's neighbour in South Africa is certainly a political question, to which we have no ready-made Christian answer. Experience has shown that the answer cannot be derived from the Church's present store of knowledge and its present forms of practice.

If the Church is preaching the Gospel, there is obviously something lacking in the Gospel, because the adherents of that Gospel are not producing the fruits by which they are supposed to be known. The Black neighbours of the White adherents have made it quite clear that they do not consider themselves to be loved. If, therefore, one believes, as I do, that there is nothing lacking in the Gospel, the only conclusion one can reach is that the Church is not in fact preaching the Gospel. The Gospel *must* be interpreted; but have we not only interpreted it but also distorted it? I believe that we have; albeit unwittingly perhaps.

I used to think that I knew what preaching the Gospel was all about. Hadn't I spent seven years being trained for this task? Wasn't I preaching 10 or 12 sermons every week (admittedly it was sometimes a matter of preaching the same sermon 10 or 12 times), and efficiently caring for the spiritual needs of a large congregation? Now I see that I am only

beginning to learn what it really means. But I would not even have begun
to learn if I had not first tried to find out what it meant in practice.

Obviously, I would not write a book myself if I did not believe that
book knowledge played some part in this learning process. But it plays
a secondary role; except in the case of one book, namely, the Bible.
Theology *is* concerned with interpreting the Bible, as traditional theology
recognises. Its task, however, is not to search the Bible for ready-made
answers to all human problems, but rather to reinterpret the Bible in the
light of different social and historical conditions. Most of us start our
adult life with some understanding of the Bible, which we have picked
up at home or at school, or perhaps even from listening to sermons.
Sooner or later we meet problems that this understanding does not equip
us to face up to. Many people then decide that the Bible, and hence
Christianity, are irrelevant to them; others cling blindly to what they
have been taught, fearing that any questioning would disturb their
spiritual security. But others realise that questions cannot be answered
before they have been asked. The earlier interpretation had been
determined by the questions that needed answering at that time; putting
new questions will therefore require a new interpretation. In this way
theology is made.

One can only theologise about one's own practice; not simply about
one's personal practice, which would be presumptuous and arrogant,
but about one's practice as part of a particular society, Church, race, etc.
This practice need not have been successful in order to provide the basis
for theological reflection. We can also, as indeed we must in South
Africa, reflect upon our failures. This book is in the first place an
attempt at such reflection. This reflection is, unavoidably, coloured by
my own personal experience, though I am not by any means proposing
that experience as a model for others.

It still causes me a little embarrassment to recall that when I first
came to South Africa nearly 18 years ago the only thing I knew about
the country was that it had a cricket team, which the England team of
that time could beat easily. For the rest I had a romantic picture of the
intrepid missionary venturing forth into Darkest Africa, prepared to
overcome all the dangers and evils which would undoubtedly beset him
on all sides, in order to preach the Gospel to the heathens. This illusion
was shattered upon my arrival. After all, Jan Smuts airport might not
compare with Heathrow but it is hardly a clearing in the jungle.
However, intrepid missionaries are not easily daunted and as we drove
towards the mission area I waited expectantly for us to leave behind the
trappings of Western civilisation. We never did.

I am not praising such naivete; nor do I regret its passing in my own
case. I am only pointing out that I did not come to South Africa with

any preconceived ideas concerning the evilness of the political system and the Christian's duty to combat it. I came purely and simply to preach the Gospel. Politics was not a problem. The people were obviously poor, but I could do my best to alleviate their condition and, more importantly, I could assure them that they would receive their reward in heaven.

I still believe that I am preaching the Gospel, though I hope that I have finally left behind some of the trappings of Western civilisation which were part of that preaching. This does not mean, of course, that one must cease to be Western in order to be Christian, but only that one must be wary of assuming that Western civilisation and Christianity are synonymous.

This Minister of Justice would doubtless have approved of my earlier efforts at preaching the Gospel, but he considered my later ones to be 'calculated to further the aims and objects of communism'. What I was saying and doing did not fit into *his* definition of Christianity; but neither did they fit into *my* definition of communism. I am a Christian and *because* I am a Christian I am a socialist. I have always had a preference, which was hereditary if not congenital, for some form of socialism, but that simply co-existed with my Christianity; whereas now a firm commitment to socialism is an integral part of my Christianity. This commitment is not the result of studying the claims of various political systems in the light of the theology I had been taught. It is the result of my experience in South Africa. I have come to see, in fact I have been *forced* to see, that any talk of, profession of belief in, or attempts at practising, love of one's neighbour are meaningless, if 'neighbour' is understood in Western, middle-class, capitalist terms.

Of course, I did not have to work all this out for myself. Other people who have had a similar experience have reflected upon this and given it a theoretical formulation and theological justification. However, such a 'theory' only really makes sense to one who has become aware of the inadequacy of his previous 'theory' when confronted with real problems about which he should, in terms of that 'theory', be concerned. If one assumes, as traditional theology does, that Christian practice has simply to be deduced from Christian 'theory' as contained in the Bible, one will never acknowledge the inadequacy of one's 'theory'. But Christian 'theory' is not the Bible; it is *our understanding* of the Bible. When we realise that our own or the Church's practice is inadequate it is not the Gospel we are questioning, but our understanding of it. We do not, therefore, look for an alternative to the Gospel, but for a new way of understanding and practising it.

As a missionary in the 'bundu', one's love of one's neighbour is usually expressed in such ways as providing not only Church services,

but also ambulance, bus, postal and various other services; it might also
extend to assisting with agricultural or other community development
projects. For some time I was happy to participate in such activities;
and I do not scorn them now. At that time I could not have acted
otherwise, because I thought that I was doing all that needed doing.
But my assessment of what was needed was based on *my* understanding
of my neighbour and of his needs, not directly on the Gospel. This
understanding took no account of political factors simply because *I* was
not aware of them, not because the Gospel excluded them.

When Mrs Shabalala came and told me that her daughter was in the
last stages of a difficult labour and needed to be taken to hospital
immediately, my response was, obviously, to take her. Everybody would
doubtless agree that that was a good and Christian thing to do and was
in no way calculated to further the aims and objects of communism. I
suppose I would eventually have come to question why I spent so much
time taking people to hospital, transporting corpses, running feeding
schemes etc, and have come to see that the underlying reason had
something to do with the prevailing political system. But for a long time
I did not see beyond the immediate human need. However, when dozens
of people came and told me that they had been given one week's notice
to sell their cattle, pack up all their belongings, and be ready to be
carted off to some unknown place, because the place where they had
been living for generations was a 'White' area; and when, further, I found
that it was not only a matter of dozens of people, but of thousands, of
hundreds of thousands, and even of millions; what then was the obvious
Christian response? To love one's neighbour? But *how*? By giving him a
blanket to keep him warm in the barren veld? One would do that much
for a stray dog. These were *people* with *human* needs. No amount of
material aid could mend their broken hearts and spirits. These people
were being, as people are still being, crushed by a political machine.
Could a Christian then say: the political factors are no concern of mine;
I'll wait until the machine has ground the people into the dust, then I'll
do my charitable work of picking up the pieces?

For many people, the obvious human and Christian response was to
try to stop the machine or at least to put a spoke in its wheel. This
response was essentially an attempt at moral persuasion. This attempt
failed, because it was based on the naive assumption that if people were
aware of the suffering caused by the policies which they implemented
or supported they would change them. I, and others who responded in
this way, should perhaps have known that this assumption was false.
But now, for me, the 'theory' that people are not changed simply by
intellectual argument has been confirmed by experience. The world is
not ruled by ideas but by people who not only form, but who are also

formed by their society. The Minister of Bantu Administration and Development knows full well what the Government's resettlement policy does to people, and he doubtless knew it before I and others spelt it out for him. But he still pursues the policy. He pursues the policy not because he is unaware of its effects or because he does not care. He does care; he cares about his own survival. And no price is too high for other people to pay for that survival. The 'resettlement' of two million people and the lack of an ambulance for Mrs Shabalala's daughter are both part of that price.

There are many people, including missionaries, who believe, apparently quite sincerely, that the fundamental causes of African poverty are ignorance - of hygiene, nutrition, agricultural methods, etc - and laziness. If these were the causes the solution, and therefore the Christian response, would be to provide education and incentives to work. If, however, one realises that the reason for people not ploughing, for example, is not laziness but the absence of the menfolk on migrant work, or that no matter how hard people worked they could not extract a living from a small patch of barren land, one sees the need for a different sort of solution, namely, a political one. In neither case can it be claimed that the solution has been deduced from the Gospel; in both cases the solution is determined by one's understanding of the causes. Nor can it be maintained that the former approach is less political; it is just as political in ignoring the political causes as the latter is in taking them into account. Whether the needs of our neighbour are in fact caused by political considerations or not is obviously a political question, not a theological one. But one must answer that question in order to decide how one is to love one's neighbour.

The experience of the inadequacy of a 'first-aid'-type charity in the face of a very real human problem made me realise that a Christian needs to do more than simply rescue people from the rubble of a broken society, in the same way as he would if they were the victims of a train smash, if his claim to love his neighbour is to have any meaning. The causes of the people's suffering in the case of the Government's resettlement policy were quite clearly political. But the more aware I became of the political implications of this policy the more clearly I saw that the policy was part of an all-embracing political system which is the root cause of virtually every evil in our society. There was no ambulance or local hospital for Mrs Shabalala's daughter because she was a 'surplus appendage' living in a 'homeland' which was not only a dumping ground and a labour pool, but which had also been exploited and impoverished for the sake of the development of the modern (White) sector.

My obligation as a Christian, therefore, is to challenge and to seek to change the whole political system. I am not saying that is all we must do.

I would not expect Mrs Shabalala's prospective grandchild to postpone his/her arrival until we have established a social order in which adequate medical facilities were provided for all. But this political task is just as obvious a Christian duty as is taking a sick person to hospital. In one's search for effective means of loving one's neighbour one experiences the need for political action and for political tools, and socialism is able to meet this need. Socialism exposes the root cause of the evils of the present system and it also challenges the basic assumption on which most 'Christian' opposition to that system is based.

The Church's opposition to the present system differs from that of other White groups only in its use of 'religious' arguments. Quite apart from the assumption that one can give religious answers to politico-economic questions, I want to ask whether these 'religious' arguments owe as much to the Gospel as they do to the assumption that Western, middle-class, capitalist values are Christian. As long as the Church remains a White middle-class institution its interests will conflict with the interests of the vast majority of its own members - Black workers and peasants. How can such a Church provide the motivation for a genuine liberation from all that is implied in South Africa by Whiteness?

The true Christian response to White domination can only come from those who suffer under that domination. As Whites we do not experience this domination, or at least we never experience it as the total, ultimate and all-pervading meaning of our lives. We are therefore in no position to tell the oppressed Black man what Christianity must mean for him. In this situation of oppression a White Church is not even in a position to interpret the Gospel. It has nothing to give, precisely because it shares 'the constant illusion of the liberal that he has something to give to the oppressed. All he has to give is further false definitions. Let the oppressed themselves say what they are . . . I would say with James Cone, the Black theologian, that where a class of people is liberating itself from the false definitions by another class, *there* is the sin of the world being overcome, *there* is the Spirit in action.' (R. Ruston, *New Blackfriars,* Feb. 1974, p.60).

The primary task of a Church which finds itself in this position is to *listen* - to listen to the voice of the oppressed and to *their* interpretation of the Gospel. But this is precisely what the 'Whiteness' of the Church does not allow it to do. It is part of the 'Whiteness' of the Church to assume that it has *the* definitive interpretation of Christianity. As I hope to show in the first part of this book, there is *no* definitive interpretation of Christianity and there never has been, not even in the Bible. Christianity is not meant to be defined; it is meant to be lived, to be made real, in every historical time and place.

I am not suggesting that Christianity can or should be interpreted in socialist rather than capitalist terms - it can *only* be interpreted by the people in the situation. Our task is to listen. But we will not be able to hear what is being said if we continue unquestioningly to accept the capitalist assumptions on which the Church's present interpretation, and hence its practice, are based. A socialist critique of our present assumptions is a necessary prerequisite for our most important task of listening to the oppressed.

There are, of course, people who quite deliberately and consciously accept the values and ideology of the ruling class. But I am concerned rather with those people who, while wishing to oppose that ideology, are unconsciously influenced by it. These, as Paulo Freire says, 'can come to renounce their idealistic illusions altogether, forsaking their uncritical adherence to the ruling class. In committing themselves to the oppressed, they begin a new period of apprenticeship.' (Quoted in *A Reader in Political Theology*, ed. Alistair Kee, p. 101.)

This book is a plea to people to lay aside their old certitudes and *begin* this 'new apprenticeship'.

Pietermaritzburg 1977

1·Theology and Politics

chapter 1
Doing is Believing

The attempts to prove either the Christianness or the un-Christianness of apartheid are both based on the assumption that Christianity can be and indeed has been defined. The only problem is to persuade people to accept this definition and to behave accordingly. This forms the basis of the Church's present approach to the problems of South African society and is, I suggest, one of the main reasons for its ineffectiveness and growing irrelevancy.

Such an approach, of its very nature, fails to take any real account of the political and social realities of the situation. It is concerned firstly with the 'truth' of its position and secondly with applying that 'truth' to a particular situation. If the situation is not in accord with this truth, as is the case in South Africa, it is assumed that this is because either the people responsible do not know the truth or else, for a variety of reasons, usually moral ones, they are not prepared to live according to it. The task of the Church, therefore, is seen to be one of educating people in the truth and exhorting them to live accordingly. While engaged in this task it is also necessary, as a work of charity, to relieve the sufferings of the victims of an unjust system by means of what Paulo Freire calls 'anaesthetic' or 'aspirin' practices. 'The basic presupposition of such action,' Freire says, 'is the illusion that the hearts of men and women can be transformed while the social structures which make those hearts "sick" are left intact and unchallenged.' ('Education, Liberation and the Church', quoted in Kee, *op.cit.*, p. 100). The social structures are not seen as having any influence either on the Church's own grasp of the truth of Christianity or on the understanding and attitudes of the people they are trying to convert. The theological conflict between the proponents and opponents of apartheid is, therefore, thought to be primarily a matter of *ideas*. It is assumed that if these ideas were changed the social structures and the whole apartheid system would also change.

This is the approach of the *reformist* as opposed to the *revolutionary*. And it is generally assumed that the Christian must be a reformist. Thus, for example, Brian Griffiths, writing about political change in any situation, can state quite categorically: 'the distinctive contribution of the Christian will be that of a reformer, a proponent of gradual change, who seeks to alter and modify the system from within.' (*Is Revolution Change?*, p. 110). Where in the Bible does one ever find it advocated that we *compromise* with a system we recognise as evil and in need of change?

One will not see the necessity of questioning the actual structures of society unless one appreciates the influence these have on one's grasp of the truth, and, therefore, even on one's understanding of Christianity. That they do have at least some influence is, I would think, accepted by most modern philosophers and theologians. This view, however, does not seem to have had any noticeable effect on the teaching and practice of the Church in South Africa. It might not seem very important that it should, but I believe that it is the failure to recognise the social and historical character both of the Christian message and of our understanding of it that is responsible for the tendency of so many churchpeople of all denominations to equate Western, capitalist, values with Christian values.

How can one explain the wide variations and even contradictions in the Church's interpretation of Christianity throughout history? For example, it seems quite obvious to most Christians today that the Bible teaches the equality of all men; yet for many centuries the Church both preached and practised inequality; in relation to slaves, women, laypeople, etc. As Roger Garaudy says, '[The] masters of Christian thought have made all class domination legitimate: slavery, serfdom, the salary system . . . [In modern times] the basic thesis [of this doctrine] will be developed in all its generality by Pope Pius X on December 18, 1903: "Human society as established by God is made up of unequal elements . . . Accordingly, it is in conformity with the order of human society as established by God that there be rulers and ruled, employers and employees, rich and poor, learned and ignorant, nobles and plebeians." ' (Quoted in L. Dewart, *The Future of Belief*, p. 202). Are we to assume that all these 'masters' were simply more ignorant of the Bible or more immoral than we are? Although they read the same Bible as we do and were just as concerned about being faithful to it as we are, they were part of a society where inequality was taken for granted; they therefore read the Bible with this assumption and we cannot blame them for coming to the conclusions they did. 'There was for well over a thousand years - and for much longer in the Roman Church - nothing in the available stock of ideas that could have led to the emancipation of

the underprivileged classes in society such as women and slaves. Treat
them in considerate manner, yes - that is clearly enough commanded in
the Scriptures. But work for their freedom? That would have been
inconceivable.' (R. Ruston, *loc.cit.*, p. 56). Even today, how can one
explain the radically different attitudes to apartheid of the Dutch
Reformed Churches in South Africa and their sister Church in Holland?
Experience has shown that these attitudes cannot be reconciled simply
by intellectual debate on the correct interpretation of Scripture. Social
and historical conditions have always had an influence upon the
understanding and practice of Christianity.

   The question of our understanding of Christianity raises the whole
question of our understanding of any truth, since, although the nature
of what we know by faith differs from other objects of our knowledge,
the *way* in which we understand is the same. There is no separate
Christian or divinely revealed way of knowing - we can only know as
human beings. As Schillebeeckx says,

> It is hardly necessary to demonstrate that the interpretation of the
> act of knowledge is also a matter of extreme importance for the
> faith. Even though religion is not in the first place a question of
> knowing but one of surrender in faith and confession, this surrender
> implies in the nature of things a consciousness of values . . . The
> critical theoretical question of how in his life and his self-
> understanding man comes into contact with the absolute is
> therefore a vital question which must precede any thematic
> exercises of his religious convictions. (*God and Man*, p. 113).

We cannot go into detail here about the philosophical nature of this
question. It is sufficient, I think, to note that the understanding of
truth upon which the present teaching and practice of the Church is
based is not a specifically Christian one. It is in fact contrary to the
Biblical understanding of truth. The Church's understanding of truth,
and more particularly of Christian truth, can be termed '*idealist*',
whereas the Biblical approach, which is radically opposed to this, can be
called '*historical*'. There are other theories too, but, generally speaking,
they have not been used as the basis for a theology.

   The idealist theory of knowledge was taken over by the medieval
scholastics from the pre-Christian Greek philosophers. There is,
therefore, nothing sacrosanct about it for the Christian and the
scholastics' assumption of it *as a philosophy* does not make it part of
the Christian faith. For the idealist, truth is absolute and objective.
Arriving at the truth is an activity of the mind, which is not influenced
by any other consideration. It has always existed and the mind has only

to discover it; once it has been discovered it cannot be changed.
'Christian truth', in this view, consists of a body of truths, which are to
be found in the Bible and, for some, also in Christian tradition. We
assent to these truths by faith. Faith is an intellectual assent which is
independent of the real person who is making it. Although we can
improve our knowledge of the truth and can apply it in different
circumstances, neither of these actions affects the truth itself.

The Bible is concerned with doing, rather than with knowing, the
truth. There is no message in the form of a series of abstract truths to
which we must give our assent. The Bible is primarily a record of *events*.
It is a report of God's actions in history: His act of creation; His
entering into covenants with His people; and most importantly, His
sending of His son, who revealed the love of the Father and made a new
covenant between God and man. It also records the response of certain
people and groups to these actions. It does not make statements which
people must first accept intellectually and then deduce from these what
they must do. The response demanded by God's action is the performance
of a particular action. The truth which is revealed by God's action is
acknowledged *by* this active response and is known *in* this response.
This, as Bonino points out, is particularly evident in the Old Testament:

> Whatever corrections may be needed, there is scarcely any doubt
> that God's Word is not understood in the Old Testament as a
> conceptual communication but as a creative event, a history-making
> pronouncement. Its truth does not consist in some correspondence
> to an idea but in its efficacy in carrying out God's promise or
> fulfilling his judgement. Correspondingly, what is required of Israel
> is not an ethical inference but an obedient participation - whether in
> action or in suffering - in God's active righteousness and mercy.
> Faith is always a concrete obedience which relies on God's promise
> and is vindicated in the act of obedience: Abraham offering his only
> son, Moses stepping into the Red Sea. There is no question of
> arriving at or possessing previously some theoretical clue. (*Doing
> Theology in a Revolutionary Situation*, p. 89).

This is also true of the New Testament. St John, for example, does not
say that you must first accept the 'truth' 'God is Love' and from that
deduce that you must therefore love your neighbour. He says rather
that only if you actually love your neighbour can you know that God is
Love, because 'A man who does not love his neighbour knows *nothing*
of God'. The statement 'God is Love' is not true for you if you are not
loving your neighbour. If you claim that it is, you are, according to John,
a liar. It is at least irrelevant whether 'God is Love' is an absolute truth,

because it cannot be known by us *except* in the action of loving our neighbour; we cannot, and we are not asked to, give a purely intellectual response to such a 'truth'. Christ's own account of the Last Judgement also makes it clear that he was not concerned with people's acceptance of doctrines, but with their practical response in feeding the hungry, visiting the sick and imprisoned, etc. 'Only he who *does* the word will know the doctrine.' (Bonino, *Doing Theology in a Revolutionary Situation,* p. 90).*

There are, particularly in the Pauline epistles, some statements which have the appearance of being absolute truths as, for example, when Paul speaks of Christ being ruler over everything (*Eph.* 1.23) or of all things being reconciled through him (*Col.* 1.20); but 'These declarations are something of an anticipation . . . The world of harmony and peace, centred wholly upon Christ, belongs to the end of time . . . The apostle is bringing the eye of prophecy to bear on the world; he is judging it by a principle, by the death and resurrection of Jesus, by that cosmic revolution which took place in its entirety in Christ, but whose effects have not yet spread out over the world' (F.X. Durrwell, C.S.S.R. *The Resurrection,* p.117). Paul does not propose such statements for his readers' intellectual assent. He is interested in how they are living according to the promise now and making it true for themselves. Thus, for example, he tells the Colossians that they have been buried with Christ (2.12); but he goes on to say: 'If you have really died with Christ to the principles of this world, why do you still let rules dictate to you?' In so far as they do let rules dictate to them it is not true that they have died with Christ.

The idealists, however, take such statements as absolute truths which we must first accept intellectually and then act in the light of. Church people in South Africa, for example, are very fond of proclaiming: 'We confess that Christ is Lord of History'. They then deduce from this that some particular government action must be condemned. But it is palpably obvious that Christ is not lord of *our* history and our *confessing* that he is will not make him such. Our history is one of oppression and exploitation, of people dying of starvation, of people being detained without trial, of children being shot by policemen. Is it of this that he is lord? There is no justification in the New Testament for making this lordship a purely spiritual matter. History is not lived in men's hearts or men's souls. We are part of a particular and very real historical situation; we can only think and speak from within this situation.

---

* For an exposition of some of the prophetic texts, in which 'to do justice *is* to know Yahweh', see J.M. Bonino, *Christians and Marxists,* pp. 31-5. For a more detailed treatment of the whole question, see Jose Miranda's *Marx and the Bible: A critique of the Philosophy of Oppression.*

If we claim to believe that Christ is Lord of this situation, what we are saying is: 'We, who in our particular situation in fact recognise the authority of the government to determine virtually every aspect of our lives, recognise only the authority of Christ.' Our practice contradicts our claim to believe that Christ is Lord of history. This belief, therefore, cannot be true, since according to the biblical understanding the truth of a belief can only be shown in action. We can only *believe* that Christ is Lord of history if we do in *fact,* not just verbally, reject any authority whose demands are contrary to those of Christ. The actual rejection in practice is part of our belief, not a consequence of it, and makes our belief true. It is then historically true, which is what the Bible is concerned about; it becomes true for us.

The Bible cannot tell us how we must make our response true. That is a political question that can only be answered in political terms, which will vary according to different social and historical conditions. Taking account of these conditions and determining their true nature, by political and sociological analysis, and acting upon such an analysis is essential for making our belief true.

A little thought will show that a theology of Christian practice that is based on an 'idealist' foundation cannot go beyond moralising about a particular situation and perhaps seeking small adjustments. Since one is only concerned with objectively applying an objective and absolute truth, one ignores the very factors that could relate such an action to the reality of the situation. But the Bible is not concerned with teaching absolute truths and our understanding of what it does teach is not purely objective. Giving my intellectual assent to truth does nothing for me or for the truth; truth is to be discovered by me in my particular social, cultural and historical condition. Whether truth does pre-exist as some absolute, eternal, abstract entity is in any event irrelevant for the Christian who wishes to base his Christian practice on the model of the Bible.

Even those Christians who seek to justify political activity directly from the Bible sometimes use this false approach. Any attempt to prove the rightness of a particular position simply by referring to biblical texts overlooks the historical nature both of the Bible and of man. Thus it is sometimes argued, for example, that since the Bible teaches that all men are one in Christ, apartheid is wrong. Discriminating between Black and White is seen as the equivalent of discriminating between Jews and Gentiles; it is therefore forbidden in virtue of Paul's teaching. But St Paul did not deduce the moral that Christians should not discriminate between Jews and Gentiles from the 'truth' that all men are one in Christ. He said that because all men are one in Christ there *is* no difference (*Gal.* 3.28). Therefore, not respecting any differences between people is the *same* as believing that all men are one in Christ.

If in practice, by apartheid, class distinction, or in other ways, we do discriminate between people, this is not simply a matter of not living up to what we believe in. It contradicts and so nullifies that belief. It is not, therefore, possible to have this belief and yet to maintain segregated schools, hospitals, or other institutions, to pay wages determined by the race of the worker, etc. That all men are one in Christ is not a theory which we can accept intellectually but fail to live up to in practice because of other circumstances such as the law of the land. In so far as we respect the law of the land in this way we thereby deny our belief.

Our practical attitude to apartheid does not follow from our belief - it determines whether or not that belief is true for us. In St Paul's time this was determined by people's attitude to Jews and Gentiles, slaves and freemen, men and women. But the nature of discrimination in our society is very different from what it was in his. Therefore, in order to make the same belief true it is necessary for us to act differently. In our society it is not enough just to ignore discrimination. It must be overcome by political means which recognise its political and economic, not only its moral, character. The Church in South Africa, however, is concerned almost exclusively about the moral implications. This is a logical consequence of an idealist approach: truth is mainly a matter of words and can only lead to more words. But words cannot make it true that all men are one. The Church's claim to believe that all men are one in Christ will only become true when it *in fact* rejects all discrimination in its own institutions and in society.

The Bible does not teach a dogmatic and a moral theology; moral obligations are not deduced from a theoretical truth. Truth is found in the response to God's demands which are revealed by his actions. As Hugo Assmann puts it: 'In the Bible . . . words have meaning only as the expression of a deed, and theory has meaning only as an expression of practice.' (*Practical Theology of Liberation,* p. 75). God does not reveal truths about Himself, or about love, or justice, or anything else. He reveals Himself. And He reveals Himself as a God of love, of justice, of salvation, of liberation. The Bible records the events by which He revealed Himself as such and how these events were given meaning by and in the response of his people. It is the historical events themselves that form the core of the Christian message. This message is not primarily a matter of doctrines; it is a report of something that happened. All doctrines are an interpretation of these events. The Bible contains the most authoritative interpretation, but it is still an interpretation. The Biblical message is not, as Schillebeeckx says,

a word from God without alloy coming down to us, as it were, vertically in a purely divine statement. God's word is given to us within the already interpretative response to it of the Old and New Testaments - believers who had found the ground of their being in God's faithfulness bore witness interpretatively to God's saving actions in Israel and in the man Jesus, the Christ, the foundation of their hope for a renewed world, and their witness was interpreted in its turn. The God of salvation was made the subject of *a conversation between men* - it was in this way that God's word was addressed to us. This human dialogue in which God gave himself to be understood was as such necessarily *situated* - it had a social setting, a living historical context. (*God the Future of Man,* p. 5).

The biblical interpretation, as we have seen, is concerned with the response to the demands that God's actions make. While it is important for us to determine more and more precisely the meaning of this response, we cannot simply take it over as our own; nor should we. We should not, because the Bible itself does not present it to us as something to accept, but as the way in which truth was realised - that is, made real - in a particular situation. For us to make the same sort of response, we must respond differently because our situation is different. We cannot simply take it over, because our understanding of that response is not simple. Nobody's understanding of the response as recorded in the Bible can be a purely objective interpretation of the text.

It is always a subject who approaches a text and who understands a text within an historical tradition and in a social and autobiographical context . . . We approach a text with presuppositions, with a preunderstanding of concepts which will be found in the text or which will be related to the contents of the text . . . we cannot come to the text with a blank mind; nor should we try. We can understand the text only in the light of the preunderstanding which we bring to the text. (Geoffrey Turner, *New Blackfriars,* June 1975, p. 275).

This applies also to the expert biblical scholars on whom most of us have to rely for assistance in interpreting the Scriptures. They do not simply use objective, scientific methods for determining the meaning of the text; even their choice of method shows a particular bias. When, therefore, we turn to the Bible for guidance about what we should do in a particular situation, we are dealing with an interpretation of an interpretation; or even an interpretation (our understanding), of an interpretation (the opinions or exegesis of experts), of an interpretation (the biblical text itself). Each of these interpretations is influenced by social, historical and other factors. Our understanding of the problem we are dealing with is likewise influenced by these factors. So we are far removed from simply giving an objective answer to an objective question. We cannot leave all these other considerations aside and find the biblical or Christian response. Such factors are part of the biblical response and must be part of any Christian response; otherwise such a response is not a human one and we, being human, can only respond in a human way. The fact that we respond in faith does not change the nature of the way in which we respond. Just as the man who says he loves God but does not love his brother is a liar, so is the man who claims to believe in God but whose practice contradicts this. Our actions, since they form part of us, are part of our act of believing. Believing is not a matter of thinking or saying; believing in God means responding to His demands. We can only respond as the particular person we are and from within our particular social and historical context; we cannot respond as a mind or a soul living in a vacuum.

To say that truth in the Bible is historical and that the understanding of this or any other truth is conditioned by other factors is not to say that everybody is free to interpret the Bible as he wishes and that the Church has therefore no authoritative message to preach.

Firstly, as we have already mentioned, any response must be an attempt to respond, in a different historical setting, with the same sort of response as the biblical response to the same events recorded there. We are seeking to respond to historical events so 'we must insist that the penetration of the original historicity of the biblical events is basic for its present demand and efficacy. Consequently, however questionable and imperfect, the critical use of the instruments that help us to reach a better understanding of this historicity is indispensable for the reflection on our Christian obedience today' (Bonino, *Doing Theology in a Revolutionary Situation*, p. 102). We must still try to find out what the Bible says, but we do this with an awareness of the presuppositions which are part of any interpretation. We can discover at least the general terms of the response demanded by the biblical events. 'They seem, in fact, to point, in their integrity and coherence, to certain directions which such concepts as liberation, righteousness, shalom, the poor, love, help us to define.' (Bonino, *op.cit.,* p. 103). (Things like helping to make the rich richer can therefore obviously be ruled out.) There is an element of theory, derived from the Bible, in our response, but we cannot find in the Bible a predetermined, absolute, theoretical justification for any particular line of action. 'At the level of theory, all that we have at our disposal, [then] , is a proportional norm - models of structurisation of faith, of which Scripture provides the first and therefore the normative ones.' (Schillebeeckx, *The Understanding of Faith,* p. 62).

Secondly, we know that the central point of the Gospel is Christ's teaching about and promise of the Kingdom. Any response must therefore be an attempt to realise, not merely to acknowledge, the values of this Kingdom. This implies using the best methods available to ensure that our understanding of the actual historical and social conditions is as objective as possible (that is, that we are consciously and critically aware of the presuppositions involved), and that the means we employ to bring about peace, justice, and love are the most effective. The Bible itself does not and cannot tell us which methods and means to use; we have to find the best way of giving practical effect to the biblical teaching on the Kingdom. The truth of our Christian response will be known by its fruits. This is the norm that Jesus himself established. He 'did not regard the truth as something we simply "uphold" or "maintain", but as something we choose to live and experience. So that our search, like his search, is primarily a search for *orthopraxis* (true practice) rather than *orthodoxy* (true doctrine). Only a true practice of the faith can verify what we believe . . . what we believe can only be made true, and be seen to be true, in the concrete results that faith achieves in the world.' (A Nolan, *Jesus Before Christianity,* pp. 139-40).

Thirdly, there is Schillebeeckx's criterion of 'acceptance by the people of God' (cf. *The Understanding of Faith,* pp. 70-2). There can be little doubt that in South Africa an interpretation and practice of Christianity that demands a direct and active political involvement of all Christians would meet this criterion. It might be rejected by many Whites, but this could easily be shown to have more to do with their politics than with their religion. Some Black Christians, because of their indoctrination in a different understanding of Christianity, might not accept it in theoretical terms, but the practice would undoubtedly be welcomed by the vast majority and the theory would follow. It is not necessary that such an interpretation be accepted by the whole Church for it to be true. The political and social conditions in other parts of the Church may be such that they demand a different response.

In determining our Christian response, therefore, we are not simply left to our own devices. We have the Biblical response as our norm, the values of the Kingdom as our goal, and the acceptance by the people of God as the test of the authenticity of our response.

However, there is no way of absolutely guaranteeing that all our actions are right; perhaps we will all be surprised at the Day of Judgement to find which of our actions are considered worthy of praise and which of condemnation. Our ultimate security lies in the fact that God loves us, not that we love Him and that we do the right things. Too much concern about the rightness of our actions betrays a lack of trust in God and a self-centred interest in our own salvation. We must be prepared, in faith, to live dangerously in our attempts to make God's love real in the world.

Because of the theoretical element in Christian practice, the Church does still have a message to preach. It cannot, however, claim that this message is derived directly from the Bible and that its preaching of it is purely objective. Unless it is prepared to acknowledge this and to question the presuppositions and assumptions which underlie its preaching and its consequent practice, it will continue to put forward a Western, middle-class, capitalist understanding of Christianity as *the* Christian message and will therefore have nothing relevant to say to the oppressed people of South Africa. Because of its assumption of the absolute nature of truth it can only moralise; because it believes that its understanding of this truth is purely objective it does not acknowledge that the norms for this moralising are more Western and capitalist than they are Christian.

In its efforts to preach a 'pure' Christianity the Church has tried to take Christianity out of the political, social and historical spheres; to remove it from the real world. It has spiritualised its content and has thus cut off the roots that Christ planted by his incarnation. The Church tries to live apart from the real world which Christ is saving and to live in an unreal realm of attitudes and intellectual beliefs, from where it looks down on the world to pass judgement. But Christianity is not all in the mind; it is revealed historically and can only be understood and practised historically. The Church's fundamentally idealist attitude is illustrated by its reaction to political events. Whenever a crisis arises, which is rather often in South Africa, Christians are urged to meet together and to ask themselves: 'what does the Gospel say about this situation?' The question should, however, be put the other way around: 'what does this situation tell us about our understanding and practice of the Gospel?'

In putting the question in the former way we are presuming, firstly, that we know what the problem is and, secondly, that the Gospels can give a solution to a problem which their authors had never heard of and could not have foreseen. The assessment of the situation is not a theological or biblical question; there is no such thing as a Christian assessment. As Christians we have to rely, like everybody else, on our own or other people's judgement about the nature and cause of the problem. Our understanding of the problem will more or less determine the answer that the Gospels give, because it will determine the questions we ask. If, for example, when faced with a crisis like the rioting in Soweto, a person, who believes that law and order is the most important thing in society, wants to find out what the Gospel says, he will look for what it says about law and order, and will find that it is basically in favour. He might then conclude that law and order must be restored at all costs: by force, consultations, making concessions, etc. Such a person might well believe that this is *the* Christian response based on the teachings of the Gospel. But it is not; it is *his* response and is based on *his* understanding of *society*.

All the Gospels can tell us is that we must love our neighbour and that at the time the Gospels were written this could be done by visiting the sick and imprisoned, feeding the hungry, clothing the naked, etc. It is fairly obvious that shooting children in the back is not an equivalent manifestation of love; but this does not help us to decide what we should do about it. That is a complex socio-political problem, on which Christian teaching throws some light and provides motivation for wanting to rectify the situation (not necessarily by restoring law and order at all costs). The best socio-political solution, which must be arrived at on these terms, *is* the Christian solution; there cannot be a separate Christian solution.

The Gospel cannot tell us very much specifically about the riots, but what do the riots tell us about our understanding and practice of the Gospel? To answer this question it is necessary to understand, as far as possible, the nature and meaning of the riots; I personally was too far removed from them really to understand. But it is clear that those involved were concerned with, among other things, the real, not just verbal, rejection of domination and they manifested a new consciousness of their power and dignity. The riots showed that people were prepared to die rather than continue with an inhuman existence. They thus taught us that this is the depth of commitment needed in this situation to give meaning to loving one's neighbour. So verbal condemnations of apartheid, community development projects, the giving of no matter what amounts of money cannot be considered adequate ways of loving one's neighbour. Such charitable actions might be sufficient in other circumstances, but not in the present South African situation. We have been taught this by these events. The Gospel warns us that we might have to lay down our lives for our brethren; the Black youth are telling us that the time for doing so is now. And they are not only *telling* us, they are *doing* it.

We know that the Gospel tells us to love our neighbour - so there is no need to ask what it says. But it does not tell us how to do it here and now. We can only learn that from the people we are supposed to be loving. It is not the Gospel message of loving our neighbour that is challenged by events such as the rioting; it is our understanding and practice of it that is being rejected. The Gospel cannot tell us how we have failed the people; but the people can tell us that we have failed the

Gospel. We have been told this repeatedly in the history of revolutions, yet the Church still seems not to understand why, 'despite all we have done for the natives', it is often one of the prime targets of revolutionary groups.

The Church in South Africa and elsewhere has no doubt sincerely tried to be loving and helpful. But its practice has been based on *its* understanding of both the problem and the solution; whereas the nature of the love demanded can only be determined by the nature of the oppression. Since this can only be understood by those experiencing the oppression, only they can determine the solution. This does not mean that we must simply listen to Blacks in the sense of consulting them about what needs to be done so that *we* can do it. Even listening to Nelson Mandela, Robert Sobukwe, Walter Sisulu, Govan Mbeki, and Steve Biko in this way would not solve the problems of South Africa. The Church's task is not to try to remove oppression, but to support the efforts of the oppressed themselves to overcome it.

These efforts, of which the rioting is one, are not to be judged by our preconceived ideas of what Christianity is; they are telling us that these preconceived ideas are wrong, because they have not led to effective love. We are not listening to them if we simply turn to these same preconceived ideas to determine our response. And this is all that we do, if we ask 'What does the Gospel say to us about this situation?' We are separating theory and practice and trying to judge somebody else's practice in the light of our theory; instead we should be asking what this practice says about both our 'theory' and 'practice'

The difference, therefore, between the 'idealist' and the 'historical' approach is not simply an academic question for a Christian. An idealist approach is bound to lead to a bias in favour of the status quo. Since the 'truth' is arrived at irrespective of social, political and historical conditions, the changing of these can only be seen as a consequence of truth and not as part of it. To adopt a specific political analysis would therefore be seen as going beyond the scope of 'Christian truth' and entering into the field of politics. The Church wishes to keep out of politics, so it can only indulge in moral condemnation and exhortation. In fact, however, in adopting this position it implicitly takes a political stance: that of the *status quo.*

The historical approach, on the other hand, since it accepts that political and other considerations are an integral part of any response, takes these explicitly into account in determining a Christian response. Only in this way can we in our present condition respond in a biblical fashion to the events proclaimed in the Bible. And it is only if we are aware of this that we can forsake a Western, middle-class, capitalist understanding of Christianity and begin to discover what Christianity means in South Africa today.

Most people, of course, do not make a conscious decision about which of these two views they hold and in practice many Christians do, fortunately, accept the latter one. Their knowledge of what is wrong with the situation comes from their personal experience of oppression. They do not first need to be given a theoretical framework. They are surrounded by an oppressive reality and seek the best means to breaking out of it - perhaps by political, cultural, or trade union activity and maybe even by rioting. All of these can be genuinely Christian responses; I am not saying that they necessarily are, but that none of them can be absolutely ruled out.

Church leaders, however, including Black ones, partly no doubt because of their Western training and perhaps partly because it is less threatening to the values of the middle class, into which the clergy are generally assimilated, tend to follow the former view. They do not, therefore, recognise the Christian character of many initiatives taken by laypeople. People accept this judgement and so conclude that the Church and Christianity are irrelevant to them. They acknowledge the clergy as the authorities on Christianity, but they are also convinced of the rightness of their own actions, so they go their own way. Hence even some Black priests are now finding themselves considered by the youth as part of the enemy. Even if Black priests did consider that such actions were a true Christian response, it is unlikely that many of them would say so in public; partly perhaps through fear of the provisions of the Terrorism Act, but also because they would know that their White colleagues, who dominate the Church, would not begin to understand what they were talking about.

chapter 2
Two Views of Salvation

The absence of a 'profound and lucid reflection on the theme of
salvation' is, according to Gustavo Gutierrez, 'one of the great
deficiencies of contemporary theology' (*A Theology of Liberation,*
p. 149). I cannot attempt to give any such reflection on salvation. Some
consideration must, however, be given to it, because a Christian's
political commitment or lack of it derives ultimately from his
understanding of salvation.

Everything depends on whether we see Christ as a personal security
blanket or as the saviour of the world; on whether we believe that we
were saved *by* Christ from the wrath of God or that we *are* saved *in*
Christ by a loving God.

Broadly speaking, we can distinguish between an 'individualist' and a
'universal' understanding of salvation. In the individualist view salvation
is seen primarily in personal terms; stress is laid on the explicit
acknowledgement of Christ as the one who saves *me* from *my* sins. By
his profession of belief in Christ the Christian comes under the 'spiritual'
rule of Christ. If he holds fast to this belief, despite the attractions of
'the world', and fulfils the religious obligations which follow from this
belief he will be rewarded in heaven. On the basis of such an
understanding of salvation, concern for one's neighbour and for the
world can only be seen either as a means of attaining one's personal
salvation or as a consequence of it.

In the universal view, on the other hand, salvation is seen as an all-
embracing process which is coextensive with creation. *Our* salvation
does not consist in acknowledging the truth of this fact, but in
participating in this process, which is at work whether anybody
acknowledges it or not. Salvation is not a separate 'religious', otherwordly activity; it is 'something which embraces all human reality,
transforms it, and leads it to its fullness in Christ: "Thus the centre of
God's salvific design is Jesus Christ, who by his death and resurrection
transforms the universe and makes it possible for man to reach
fulfillment as a human being. This fulfillment embraces every aspect of
humanity: body and spirit, individual and society, person and cosmos,

time and eternity. Christ, the image of the Father and the perfect God-Man, takes on all the dimensions of human existence." ' (Gutierrez, *op. cit.,* pp. 51-2). By 'universal' salvation, therefore, we do not mean that everybody is saved willy-nilly, but that salvation is available to all and in every activity.

A personal commitment to Christ is obviously essential for anyone who calls himself a Christian, but this commitment must be that of a real person - a social and political being, living in a real historical situation. And it must be a commitment to the Christ, not to a devotional Jesus. Such a commitment cannot be a private arrangement between two individuals. We are neither private nor individuals; we are part both of mankind and of a new mankind. And Christ has so identified himself with all men that we cannot have a relationship with him without at the same time being related to all men. It is the greatest arrogance, to say the least, to try to appropriate salvation to oneself as a private possession and it implies the rejection of salvation as a gift. 'Christianity,' as Paul Ramsey has said, 'is the negation of the general religious desire for salvation as the supreme personal value to be gained.' (*Basic Christian Ethics,* p. 151).

No Christian would wish to detract from or to gloss over what Christ physically did on earth. But we cannot separate this aspect from the whole and make a religion for ourselves out of it. 'Christian theology begins and ends with Christ. Christ is not a further extra for those who want a fancier religion for themselves . . . through the blood of the cross God is reconciling to himself the whole universe, the whole scheme of things which was inaugurated in the Genesis activity.' (J. D. Davies, *Beginning Now,* pp. 14-15).

Christ's actual sufferings were not the beginning and end of the matter of salvation; he himself is. It is not, therefore, completely true to say, as John Stott does: 'There is healing through his wounds, life through his death, pardon through his pain, salvation through his suffering.' (*Basic Christianity,* p. 99). There is; but such a statement implies that the efficacy of Christ's saving work derives from the *intensity* of his sufferings. His sufferings were contingent upon men's sin, but his work of salvation, of bringing all things and particularly man as the centre of creation to fulfillment, is independent of man's sin because 'In Christ He [God] chose us *before the world was founded,* to be dedicated, to be without blemish in His sight, to be full of love; and He destined us - such was his will and pleasure - to be accepted as His sons through Jesus Christ.' (*Eph.* 1.4-5).

Christ came to enable man to be *fully* in communion with God. But, because of man's sin, this communion needed not only to be fulfilled but to be restored. To restore it his death was necessary, because he 'became sin' for our sake and 'the wages of sin is death'. To see Christ primarily, almost exclusively, as a redeemer from personal sin, as the individualist does, is to make the contingent event of man's sin the centre of Christianity and not Christ himself. The whole of creation revolves around Christ, not around sin.

We as Christians believe that God created the world and all that is in it. In this world there are now nearly 4,000 million people. Some two-thirds of these people lack the basic requirements for a human existence; millions are starving; millions upon millions are being exploited, oppressed, tortured, and killed. Do we have nothing more to say to these people than 'Christ has saved you from your sins'? Have we no more consolation to offer to a mother, whose own body is so shrivelled from hunger that she has nothing to give her baby who is dying of starvation, than to tell her not to be 'unduly burdened by the trials and sorrows of this present life, remembering that it is if we suffer with Christ that we shall also be glorified with him' (Stott, *op.cit.,* pp. 143-4). Or, as Peter de Rosa asks,

> What message has Christianity for the splendid, technologically advancing world in which our children are being brought up and of which they are justly proud? Is Christianity's only task to make scientists - those who really 'unite the world' - more loving and Christlike? Would not this be to fob off Christ with a rather trivial role? - as if the world goes on under its own powers and is influenced only indirectly by Christ when he shares his holiness with men. Isn't Christ more central to the progress of history than that? Isn't he the man for whom the world was made, the one whom God had in mind when countless ages ago the cosmos first sprang into being? Doesn't the world progress to unification and perfection by reason of this influence? (*Christ and Original Sin,* p. 128).

These questions can only be answered in the affirmative if salvation is something more than deliverance from personal sins and from an evil world. And, according to the Bible, it is. God 'has made known to us His hidden purpose . . . namely, that the universe, all in heaven and on earth, might be brought into a unity in Christ' (*Eph.* 1.9-10). 'His [Christ's] is the primacy over all created things. In him everything in heaven and on earth, was created . . . the whole universe has been created through him and for him . . . all things are held together in him.' (*Col.* 1.15-17). There are numerous other texts which make explicit what is the theme of the whole Bible. In the Old Testament the God who creates is the God who saves. 'The character of God is known primarily not from creation but from Exodus. The character of the God of Exodus, the

God of the covenants, is read back into the creation story.' (Davies, *op. cit.,* p. 14). Throughout the Old Testament the Creator reveals himself as a God who saves in history. In the New Testament this saving activity becomes a re-creation. 'Our Saviour does not come to save us *from* creation, for he who creates us is not to be separated from him who saves us. It is wrong to teach that loving Son delivers us from angry Father; equally it is wrong to think that spiritual Saviour delivers us from the traps of physical Creator.' (Davies, *op.cit.,* p. 20).

Christ's saving work cannot be restricted, therefore, to forgiving the sins of those who acknowledge him as their saviour. Salvation is available to all men in all their actions. It is not reserved for the privileged 'religious' few, as the individualists would have it. Such an individualist view is starkly stated by Stott, who writes: 'Are not all people the children of God? No! The Bible clearly distinguishes between a general paternity of God which extends over all whom He has made, and a restricted fatherhood which is enjoyed by those whom He has remade in Christ. He is the Creator of all; but He is the Father only of those who have trusted in Jesus Christ as their Saviour.' He claims that this is clear from St John's prologue and concludes: 'The children of God are those who are born of God; and those who are born of God are those who have received Christ into their lives and who have believed in His name.' (Stott, *op.cit.,* pp. 133-4).

This would seem directly to contradict Christ's own teaching about salvation contained in his account of the Judgement (*Mt.* 25, 31-46). Those who were saved had to ask: when did we see you hungry, thirsty, naked, in prison? It was what they did that was important. And what they did was unknowingly accept salvation by accepting their brother. It is not our acknowledgement of salvation that makes it present; it is already there. We can only accept it; sometimes consciously and explicitly, more often unconsciously, in loving our brother, which as St Augustine says, is the *only* thing a 'person cannot do and still be wicked'.

An 'individualist' understanding of Christ as my personal deliverer from sin and from the evils of the world takes salvation out of its Biblical context and reduces Christianity to the level of a salvation myth. Bonhoeffer explains the unbiblical nature of this approach far better than I could hope to do. He writes:

> Unlike the other oriental religions the faith of the Old Testament is not a religion of salvation. Christianity, it is true, has always been regarded as a religion of salvation. But isn't this a cardinal error, which divorces Christ from the Old Testament and interprets him in the light of the myths of salvation? . . . The Old Testament speaks of *historical* redemption, i.e. redemption on this side of death, whereas

the myths of salvation are concerned to offer men deliverance from death. Israel is redeemed out of Egypt in order to live before God on earth. The salvation myths deny history in the interests of an eternity after death ... It is said that the distinctive feature of Christianity is its proclamation of the resurrection hope, and that this means the establishment of a genuine religion of salvation, in the sense of release from this world. The emphasis falls on the far side of the boundary drawn by death. But this seems to me to be just the mistake and the danger. Salvation means salvation from cares and need, from fears and longing, from sin and death into a better world beyond the grave. But is this really the distinctive feature of Christianity as proclaimed in the Gospels and in St Paul? I am sure it is not. The difference between the Christian hope of resurrection and a mythological hope is that a Christian hope sends a man back to his life on earth in a wholly new way ... The Christian, unlike the devotees of the salvation myths does not need a last refuge in the eternal from earthly tasks and difficulties. (*Letters and Papers From Prison,* Fontana edition, p. 112).

In a salvation myth, the hero rescues his followers from evil powers and provides a refuge for them. Christ did not do that; he overcame the powers of evil and so made it possible for us to overcome them now. 'Heaven' is not a place for those who cannot cope with the world; nor does it provide a motivation for our efforts to cope. It is the consequence and fulfilment of our *present* participation in the historical process of salvation. 'Salvation as a typical religious category is ultimately the actual encounter between God and man in mutual trust, because man's freedom to make history his salvation comes about only in historicity.' (Schillebeeckx, *God and Man,* p. 30). 'Heaven' is the fulness of this encounter, which takes place in *this* transformed cosmos, which is the Kingdom. The Kingdom is not another word for heaven. In the Kingdom we will be with God, and 'being with God' is what heaven is. What exactly happens in the meantime (I suppose we cannot really speak of a 'meantime') we just do not know. We believe that we will be 'with God' in some way, but we do not know how. A Christian, however, should be more concerned with 'life after birth' than with life after death (again, one cannot really speak of 'after'). Salvation is essentially about this world; about its present and its future. Christ himself told us very little about heaven - when he used the actual word it was usually as another name for God - and he certainly did not propose it as a 'last refuge'; nor did he hold it out as a bait.

There are probably few, if any, people who take literally the pious and rather boring images of heaven and the gruesome descriptions of hell, which were the stock-in-trade of the fire and brimstone school of preachers, no more than they believe that God really is an old man with a long white beard. We can only use imagery and symbols about such matters, but the trouble with the old images was that they were described in such graphic detail and were the subject of such impassioned rhetoric that the preachers themselves appeared to forget, and their audiences had probably never been told, that they were not meant to be taken literally. Although much of the imagery has been discarded, the belief and practice of many Christians is still influenced by the crude idea which it conveyed of heaven as another world which awaited those who managed to remain uncontaminated by this one. It is still true of some that concern about heaven detracts from concern about the present world, which is seen simply as a testing ground for the real life, which is to come. Such an approach, however, implies that God made a mistake in creating men and the world and that Christ's victory was an empty one.

There is much truth in the old legend of the saint who met an angel carrying a flaming torch in one hand and a pail of water in the other. When asked what they were for, the angel replied, 'The torch is to burn down the castles of heaven and the water is to put out the flames of hell and then we shall see who really loves God.' (Quoted in Dewart, *op. cit.,* p. 36). And, he could have added, who really loves man.

Belief in heaven, as the Vatican Council stresses (*Gaudium et Spes* N. 41), far from detracting from our concern with the present world, should give added meaning to our involvement. It does not give this meaning by *motivating* us to do good or to love our neighbour. We cannot love our neighbour *in order* to get to heaven; that would not be the disinterested love that Christ demands. Christ did not promise us heaven as a reward for doing what we are told. He gave us his assurance that 'heaven' - being with God - is the natural consequence of being with Him now by loving our neighbour. Heaven begins now and if it does not begin now it can never reach fulfilment for us. But it cannot be begun now by cutting oneself off from 'the world' and other people in order to concentrate on one's own personal salvation, since it is precisely in the world and in relationship with other people that salvation is to be found. 'What ultimately matters is the person I become and the persons my fellow men become through our actions in the world in community with each other. The richer one becomes as a person in this life, the richer is one's eternal destiny. All cultural activity has an eternal significance, be it scientific or artistic, intellectual or practical. Everything that enriches one as a person enters into one's destiny.' (M. Simpson, S.J., *Death and Eternal Life*, p. 92).

We cannot be saved as individuals, because being in relationship with

others is an essential part of being human, and being in loving
relationship with others is essential to being a Christian. A relationship
is not loving if it is entered into for some ulterior motive - even the
motive of 'getting to heaven'. 'Jesus tries to motivate us to love one
another not by offering rewards or threatening punishments, but by
awakening in us the faith or strong conviction that God loves all men.'
(Nolan).* We have this faith only if we do in fact love all men, and if we
do, we also have the assurance that Christ's promise will be fulfilled.

There is no way in which we can *earn* heaven, but Christ has promised
that God *gives* it to those who love their neighbour. It is, therefore, our
present love for all men that is important. This is the message that Christ
emphasised by his proclamation of, and concern for, the coming of the
Kingdom, the future of this world. Far from offering us an avenue of
escape from this world, Christ gives us the task of 'making it into the
heavenly social environment' (Schillebeeckx, *World and Church*, p. 11).

The reduction of Christianity to a 'salvation myth' arises, at least in
part, from our projecting our idea of forgiveness and salvation on to
God rather than changing our ideas in the light of what the Bible tells us
about God's actions. Like Martin Elginbrodde, we pray:

Hae mercy o' my soul, Lord God;
As I wod do, were I Lord God,
And ye were Martin Elginbrodde.

If we were offended we would probably become angry and seek
retribution. We therefore presume that God acts in the same way. On
this presumption a whole theology of redemption has been built up.
This theology states that Christ effected our salvation by counter-
balancing the evil of Adam's sin by his suffering and death. God was so
angered by Adam's sin that it took an infinite amount of reparation to
appease him; therefore, only His son, being God, could do it. In
effecting this reparation he merited an infinite amount of grace which
we can now draw on through the sacraments, prayer, and other religious
acts. This is the sort of theology on which I was brought up and which I
still hear in sermons. It is not, however, peculiar to the Roman Church.
The official teaching of the Anglican Church as contained in the 39
articles, for example, states: '[Christ] truly suffered, was crucified, dead
and buried, to reconcile his Father to us.' This is the exact opposite of
what St Paul teaches: 'From first to last this has been the work of God.
He has reconciled us men to himself through Christ, and He has enlisted
us in this service of reconciliation. What I mean is, that God was in

* Quoted from an unpublished lecture

Christ reconciling the world to Himself.' (*2 Cor.* 5.18-19).

Such an understanding of salvation clearly implies a separation, even an antipathy, between the God who saves and the God who creates. We need a saviour to protect us from the creator whose work we have messed up; we need Christ to shield us both from God and from the world. But, according to Scripture, God is on our side; and He always has been. Christ did not come simply to patch up what had gone wrong; he came to bring the original creation to fulfilment: 'Human sin never changed God's mind. God's major attribute in the Old Testament is His fidelity . . . We should like to go a step further, according to a truly biblical, patristic and Franciscan tradition, and say that from the very beginning the whole cosmos, and humanity in it, was created to be united in Christ, and therefore is inwardly and dynamically directed towards Christ, as its full realisation and perfection.' (Piet Fransen, *Intelligent Theology*, vol III, p. 168).

Salvation cannot be opposed to creation, nor superimposed on it, nor placed alongside it. Salvation is the transformation of the whole of creation in Christ through whom 'all things came to be'. It is the fulfilment of God's original purpose: the communion of all men with Him and with one another. But all men are not one either with God or with one another. It follows that salvation is something which has not yet happened. 'We have been saved, though only in hope.' (*Rom.* 8.24). We cannot therefore possess salvation or acknowledge it as something that has already happened. Our ultimate salvation lies in the future; though not in the sense that a piece of cloud has been set aside for us and our names attached to a harp. It is a future that has been made present in Christ and because of him it can be made present for us.

Salvation, from God's point of view as it were, is His Kingdom, the restoration of all men and all creation to communion with Him which will be fully realised with the final establishment of the Kingdom. For us it is the anticipation of this future. We anticipate it by giving practical effect to the values of the Kingdom. 'Where-ever the message of the imminent Kingdom of God is accepted, God has already come into power and man now has communion with God. The salvation which is communion with God requires nothing else than to accept the message of the imminent Kingdom of God now.' (W. Pannenberg, *Theology and the Kingdom of God*, p. 65).

God has accepted us in Christ and we are saved by accepting this acceptance. God's acceptance is revealed to us as a promise of fulfilment for the whole of creation in the Kingdom. Our acceptance of this is something very different from what the individualist means when he says that he acknowledges Christ as his saviour. Such an acknowledgement is simply an activity of the mind giving its assent to a 'truth'; whereas acceptance means that the Christian 'has to make this believed promise come true in history and has to do this precisely by making this history *now*' (Schillebeeckx, *God the Future of Man*, p. 183). The former can only elicit a spiritual and otherwordly response; the latter demands a human and this-wordly one, because it is people and this world to whom God offers salvation. Bonhoeffer defines such a response as 'living unreservedly in life's duties, problems, successes, failures. In so doing we thrown ourselves completely into the arms of God, taking seriously not our own suffering, but those of God in the world.' The individualist, however, seeks to escape from the world and to respond by 'religious' action.

The difference between the two responses is seen not only in the larger political sphere but also in everyday activity. A person who rises at 2 a.m. to pray is considered a very ascetic and virtuous person; but the parent who gets up at 2 a.m., 3 a.m. and 4 a.m. to feed or change a baby is only doing his/her duty. I can vouch for it from personal experience that there is far more opportunity for the self-denial so lauded by the 'religious' in marriage than there is in a monastery. One spends far more time in silence and solitude when under house arrest than when living in a Religious House. If we are truly concerned for others we do not need artificial means of sharing in the sufferings of Christ. In South Africa, particularly, the government provides very real means of doing this. A 'this-wordly' response, therefore, is not an easy way out, a soft life. It is a real and historical response to a real and historical process of salvation and means really sharing in Christ's sufferings instead of just thinking and praying about them. It means actually sharing one's food with the hungry rather than piously remembering 'all those who are hungry' before tucking in to a large meal. Surely David Russell's living for six months on the same meagre diet as the people of Dimbaza, in order to draw attention to their needs and to identify himself with the people who were suffering, was a far more meaningful and Christian action than any Lenten fast undertaken for the good of one's soul?

Fortunately, most people love someone and this is quite literally their saving feature. In so far as 'religion' detracts from this loving activity or involves the rejection of any part of God's creation it is a hindrance not a help to salvation. To pass by on the other side because you are going to church is to reject salvation in the name of 'religion'.

We might seem to have wandered far from the theme of political involvement; but I don't think we have. It is this all-embracing nature of Christ's saving work which gives meaning, motivation, and depth to our involvement. We are not asked to withdraw from the world and to devote ourselves to the cultivation of a 'salvation myth'. Our place at the centre of creation and our task of dominating the earth has been restored to us. This task necessarily entails political action because it is political structures that divide men and exploit rather than dominate the earth. To cut ourselves off from political involvement is to cut ourselves off from salvation. To seek to escape from this task into 'religion' is to make human history no more than a divine puppet show. To fulfil it is to be both human and Christian. As Gutierrez says,

> when we assert that man fulfils himself by continuing the work of creation by means of his labour, we are saying that he places himself, by this very fact, within an all-embracing salvific process. To work, to transform this world, is to struggle against misery and exploitation and to build a just society is already to be part of the saving action, which is moving towards its complete fulfilment. All this means that building the temporal city is not simply a stage of 'humanization' or 'pre-evangelization' as was held in theology up until a few years ago. Rather it is to become part of a saving process which embraces the whole of man and all human history. (*op.cit.,* pp. 159-60).

Since this saving process is not complete, it is true that 'life on earth is all a warfare'. But it is not a warfare between body and soul, material and spiritual, this world and the world to come. It is a struggle between good and evil, justice and injustice, the human and the inhuman; in other words, between salvation, which unites, and sin, which divides. In today's world the division of men is enshrined in political ideologies and perpetuated by political and social structures. Such structures are the concrete manifestation of sin. Discrimination and exploitation are not simply the result of sin; they *are* sin. I am not saying that that is all sin is, but that is where it is most evident and most divisive. These sinful structures constitute 'the world' that Christians have to reject. The world of apartheid, the world of exploitation and oppression are the enemy, not the physical universe. Perhaps the youth of Soweto were acting on a literal understanding of the sinfulness of the actual structures of oppression when they burned down Bantu Administration Board offices.

After 2,000 years of Christianity we do not seem to have made very much progress in uniting men with God and with one another. But we have Christ's word for it that it will happen. Shouldn't we then just stand aside from the present conflict and prepare ourselves for his coming? If it is all going to come right in the end, why should we bother about doing anything more than keeping our own noses clean in the meantime? Because we are not saved *from* this world, but *in* it and *with* it. Christ did not save us from drowning by standing on the bank and throwing us a life-belt; he jumped in and taught us how to swim. The future has, in Christ, broken into the present. Christ has not, having made his brief appearance on the stage of human history, withdrawn to some place outside time from where he watches the world go by. He has gone on ahead and 'draws all things to himself'. This is the basis of our hope.

Hope looks to the future not to the past. We do not simply await and long for a future Kingdom; we hope for it. And we 'give account for this hope that is in' us (*1 Pet.* 3.15) by realising the future in the present by working 'to hasten it on' (*2 Pet.* 3.12). This future is the Kingdom of God, which Christ spoke of both as coming and as having come.

That the Kingdom of God was the centre of Christ's teaching can hardly be questioned. What exactly he meant by it has, however, been subjected to a variety of interpretations. At one extreme it is identified with heaven and can be present in this world only in men's hearts; at the other, there is a tendency to identify its final manifestations with a future Socialist Republic of Azania. The one 'spiritualises' Christ's teaching; the other over-simplifies it. The Kingdom is not present in us or in any particular form of society.

Since salvation is not a purely spiritual and otherwordly activity, the culmination of God's saving activity in the establishment of the Kingdom cannot be understood as a purely spiritual and otherwordly activity. Such an understanding denies any validity to political activity, except as a demand of 'charity'. But to provide a motivation for and to stress the importance of our commitment to the bringing about of a better society it is not necessary nor permissible to go to the other extreme, as some proponents of a 'Social Gospel' have done, and to identify the improvement of society with the building up of the Kingdom of God. 'The coming of the Kingdom will involve cosmic revolutions and change far beyond anything conceivable as a consequence of man's progressive labour. God will establish his Kingdom unilaterally . . . This future is expected to come in a marvellous way from God himself; it is not simply the development of human history or the achievement of God-fearing men.' (Pannenberg, *op.cit.,* p. 52). But, as Pannenberg continues, 'God's rule is not simply in the future, leaving men to do nothing but wait quietly for its arrival. No, it is a mark of Jesus' proclamation of the Kingdom of God that future and present are inextricably interwoven. To understand this interrelation is one of the most problematic questions in contemporary study of Jesus' teaching.' (p 53).

The precise nature of the relationship between our present activity and the future Kingdom is still the subject of theological debate. This is not the place to attempt a full-scale exposition of this 'problematic

question'. I think it is sufficient to state here what is clear and to leave
the problematic areas to the theologians, whose task it is to clarify the
how and the why of what ordinary Christians know almost intuitively to
be right. In doing this we are in the respectable, if not very radical,
company of the Vatican Council, which satisfied itself with saying, 'The
renovation of the world . . . is in a sense really anticipated in this world.'
(*Constitution on the Church*). That it is anticipated is not questioned;
all that is open to question is the sense in which this anticipation is real.

We can say that we make the Kingdom present by living according to
the values of the Kingdom, but this does not mean that we must
pretend that the Kingdom has arrived or that we can set aside some
corner of a foreign world that is forever the Kingdom. The Kingdom has
not arrived; nor will its coming be a gradual process. We do not make it
present *as* an an historical reality; but we do make it present *in* historical
reality. We do not build the Kingdom, we build the world. But because
of the meaning and efficacy given to our actions by salvation in Christ
these are not two separate activities; they are present in one act. Thus it
is true to say, as Gutierrez does, that 'the growth of the Kingdom is a
process which occurs historically *in* liberation, in so far as liberation
means a greater fulfilment of man' (*op.cit.,* p. 177). But it would not be
true to say that this occurs *by* liberation.

Making the Kingdom present is not a question of making a future
place become a present *place*. The Kingdom is not future to the world
in the sense of being beyond or outside it; it is the future *of* the world.
It is not a new creation or a new salvation. The power which will effect
the final transformation is the same power that is already at work in
man. 'Where Christ rules the Kingdom of God is already dawning.'
(Pannenberg, *op.cit.,* p. 77). This 'power' is not simply an interior
spiritual quality in men's hearts. It is given historical form in human
historical forms. Such forms do not then become parts of the Kingdom
in a spatial sense; but they do become in a very real sense 'of the
Kingdom'. How this can happen we do not know, no more than we can
know how Christ can be both God and man; but that it happens we do
know. If for no other reason, we know because whatever we do for the
least of his little ones, we do for Christ. It is not *like* doing it for him; it
is not *as if* we do it for him. We do it, whether we are aware of the fact
or not. What we do for man we do for God. What we do for the
liberation of man we do for the Kingdom of God.

Many Christians are probably satisfied with an understanding of the
Kingdom which does not go beyond saying, 'I believe it is going to come
and in the meantime I must do my bit.' The exact relationship between
his 'bit' and the coming Kingdom does not really concern him. And it is
true that doing one's bit is more important than all the theologising.

However, this 'bit' has become so individualised and spiritualised that, in practice, it often implies a denial of belief in the universality of salvation and in the coming of the Kingdom.

Those who understand the Kingdom in a spiritual and otherwordly sense rely heavily on two biblical texts in particular, namely, the old mistranslation of *Luke* 17.21: 'The Kingdom of God is within you', and *John* 18.36: 'My Kingdom is not of this world'. It is now agreed by biblical scholars that both because of the word used and because of the context the former text should be translated: 'The Kingdom of God is *among* you'. Regarding the latter text, no one would maintain that the Kingdom is of this world; it is by definition of God. But since God has come into the world, His Kingdom can, and will be, *in* this world. After reviewing the biblical evidence in some detail, Albert Nolan concludes: 'The fact that his [Jesus'] way of speaking about the Kingdom is based upon the pictorial image of a house, a city or a community leaves no doubt about what he had in mind: a politically structured society of people here on earth ... Nothing that Jesus ever said would lead one to think that he might have used this term in a nonpolitical sense.' (*op.cit.*, pp. 47-8).

I do not believe, however, that it was these texts which led people to understand the Kingdom in spiritual terms; I think it was the other way around. It was their presuppositions about the spiritual nature of everything connected with 'religion' which led them to read such an interpretation into the texts. Translators who were part of a society which believed that God was only interested in 'souls', because the 'soul' is the superior part of man, would probably not even have thought of consulting a lexicon about the meaning of the word for 'within' or 'among'. Those who 'spiritualise' salvation must necessarily 'spiritualise' the Kingdom. Even if such people were forced, on linguistic grounds, to admit that the word used by Luke meant 'among' and not 'within', they would not necessarily change their ideas about the nature of the Kingdom.

The difference between the understanding of salvation and the Kingdom in spiritual terms, which follows from the individualist view, and an historical understanding does not lie simply in the content of belief. It is not just a matter of one side saying the Bible says one thing and the other saying that it says something else. There is also the question of how we understand what we claim the Bible says. The Bible tells us that God saves man. It does not define any of these words; it describes them. But under the influence of an 'idealist' Greek philosophy, we insist on defining everything. So we read the account of salvation in the Bible with a preconceived idea about the one who gives it and the one who receives it; as we have seen, we also intrude a legalistic conception of salvation. We thus arrive at our understanding of what the Bible says. Then, if we are 'idealists' we give our intellectual assent to this and draw some practical, moral conclusions. We understand our response as spiritual because we understand salvation as spiritual, but we only understand salvation as spiritual because we started from an understanding of ourselves as essentially spiritual. We have only used the Bible to confirm what we already knew about the meaning of 'God saves man'. The point at which to break into this circle is at the understanding of 'man', by substituting a biblical and historical understanding of man for a Greek one. If man is saved and man is essentially historical, he must be saved historically and he must respond historically. This, as we have seen, is what he does in the Bible. In this view our preconceived ideas are critically examined in the light of the Bible; in the 'idealist' view they are not even acknowledged. If the Greek understanding of man and of God is correct then we can 'spiritualise' just about everything the Bible says and we can only expect a 'spiritual' Kingdom. But such a Kingdom would not be the Kingdom of the God of the Bible and it would not be man who was looking forward to it.

Whatever the Bible says about salvation, if we understand this in 'idealist' terms of 'truths' to which we must give our intellectual assent, we will understand the promise of the Kingdom and our response to it in 'spiritual' terms. It would be possible for an 'idealist' to acknowledge the truth of all that we have said about the nature of salvation and of the Kingdom and yet still see his response as primarily a 'spiritual' matter. He might say, yes, that's true, so I must be more concerned about the whole man and the whole world. But the important thing would be that it was 'true': any action that might follow would be secondary. In fact, the more he acknowledged the truth of it the more time he might spend in contemplating that 'truth'.

Truth in the Bible, however, as we have already seen, is not something to be contemplated; it is to be done. The Bible is not concerned simply with a *doctrine* of salvation. It describes the historical process of salvation and demands that *we* - not 'minds' or 'souls' - respond. Our belief in the biblical doctrine of salvation - which arises from reflection on God's actions and man's response - only becomes true in so far as we make this response. We do not believe that salvation is the transformation of all men and of the whole universe culminating in the establishment on earth of the Kingdom of God if we are not working now for this transformation.

Our working for it would have no meaning if the Bible had not assured us that this is what salvation is and that it would ultimately overcome all obstacles. On the other hand, the biblical assurance means nothing *for us* if we do not respond in this way. In other words, biblical exegesis can establish what the object of Christ's promise is, namely, that he will establish his Kingdom on earth and not simply in men's hearts, but the promise is not realised by our agreeing that this is what the Bible says. The Bible does not ask for our agreement; it demands our response. Our activity is not a consequence of our agreement; it is part of our response.

This response is one of acceptance, because salvation and the Kingdom are gifts; rather, they are one gift. We cannot demand a gift or force it to be given. On the other hand, a gift cannot be forced *on* anyone, nor can it be a reward that is earned. Our task, therefore, is to make ourselves and all men open to the reception of this gift. We do not have to make ourselves acceptable to God so that He can reward us with the Kingdom. God, through Christ, has already made us acceptable. The trouble is that we have not accepted His acceptance of us.

The Kingdom can only come for those who are prepared to accept it. In this sense it is true to say that we *prepare* for the coming of the Kingdom. This does not mean that we build up the Kingdom in piecemeal fashion or that once we have made a certain amount of progress God steps in and puts the finishing touches to it; the Kingdom is not the cherry on the top of an otherwise perfect cake. Nor does it mean that we necessarily make unfettered progress towards the Kingdom. Sometimes, as could well be the case in South Africa today, we move further away from it.

Our preparation is not a selfish individualistic pursuit; we *share* in the Kingdom, we do not each have our own. It is the Kingdom we are to be concerned about, not ourselves. We must therefore also lead other men to believe in the coming of the Kingdom. We do not give them this faith, but we do make them able to accept it. A man cannot really want something unless he already knows it. If you did not know that there was such a thing as a banana, you could not want one. If someone told you about the existence of something called 'bananas', this might make you curious but it could not arouse a desire to eat one. The desire might be aroused if the person went on to give a vivid description of how delicious bananas were. But the description could only be vivid if it were given in terms of something else that you had already tasted. It would not help to say that they were better than peaches, if you had never tasted peaches either. In the same way, men can only desire the coming of the Kingdom if they have already experienced something of what it is like. Since knowledge is not simply an activity of the mind, men cannot know what the Kingdom is like just by being told 'truths' about it. They can only know if they experience it in a real historical context.

We do not know exactly what the Kingdom will be like, because

'what we shall be has not yet been disclosed' (*1 Jn* 3.2). We speak of it
as a 'society' in much the same way as we speak of God as a 'person'.
Christ described it in this way and spoke of it as a kingdom where
justice, peace and brotherhood would reign. We only believe this if we
are working now for these values; and others can only be led to believe
if they experience our efforts for justice, peace and brotherhood. In
other words, political action, which is the only means by which these
values can be implemented and experienced now, is necessary both to
make our own faith true and to make it credible for others. This,
however, is not simply a task that has been given to us to keep us
occupied until the preordained time for the coming of the Kingdom
arrives. If this were the case, there would be no explanation for Christ's
insistence on the imminence of the coming of the Kingdom and for the
urgency of his call to repentance.*

    Christ preached: 'Repent for the Kingdom of God is at hand.' His
hearers did not repent and the Kingdom did not come. If they had
repented they would not have *caused* the Kingdom to come, but their
failure to repent prevented it from coming. 'To repent' meant to
change their ways completely and to live by the values of the Kingdom
instead of according to 'the law' and the pursuit of their own selfish and
nationalist interests. Jesus did not try to bring about this change in
people by presenting them with 'truths' or intellectual arguments. He
asked people to believe in him rather than in the persuasive power of
his words. 'Faith was an attitude that people caught from Jesus through
their contact with him, almost as if it were a kind of infection. It could
not be taught, it could only be caught.' (Nolan, *op.cit.,* p. 32). In effect
he was saying: 'here is the Kingdom of God - the blind recover their
sight, the lame walk, the lepers are clear, the deaf hear, the dead are
raised to life, and the poor are hearing the good news. Accept it by
changing your ways, or reject it by continuing in your present ways'.
'What he wanted to do most of all was to awaken the same compassion
and the same faith in the people around him. That alone would enable
the power of God to become operative and effective in their midst.'
(Nolan, *op.cit.,* p. 36).

    Christ was more interested in liberating people than in talking about
liberation. To be liberated meant to put man above the law; not to lord
authority over others but to serve; to show love and compassion. This is
what he did and this is what he wanted others to do. He did not want
them to respond by saying how marvellous he was or by calling him
'Lord'. They could not enjoy the same freedom and show the same love
and compassion as he did unless they had faith; but, on the other hand,

---

*   cf. Nolan, *op.cit.,* particularly chapter 12.

the failure to show love and compassion prevented them from having faith. The faith that Jesus was trying to awaken was a believing-active response to God's liberating power that was at work in him. The Kingdom was imminent because only the need for this response stood between its coming and the then present state of affairs. The response was not given, so the Kingdom did not come.

The Kingdom is still imminent, but the response still has not been given, so the Kingdom still has not come. Instead of continuing the task of awakening faith in the Kingdom by making it present, Christianity in its institutional forms has tended to turn Christ into no more than an example, albeit the supreme one, of moral virtue and even worse into an idol of the past, around which it has constructed a 'religion' with marked similarities to that of the Pharisees. It is a static religion in which we wait for Christ's coming rather than prepare for it. The Jews of Christ's time were waiting for the Kingdom, but that was not enough to make people ready for it to come. Neither is it for us. To have faith and to awaken faith in the coming of the Kingdom means to make God's liberating power real, as Christ did.

Since Christ's time the obstacles to this power have increased. Christ liberated the people of his time from the things that bound them at that time: 'the Law', 'religion', mental and physical disease. To liberate man today means freeing him from national and international exploitation, which can only be done by political means. This is not to set political means over against the power of God or of the Kingdom; it is this power which is released through these means. 'We are not called to choose between concern for the Kingdom and concern for society. Rather, in concern for society we are concerned for its end and destiny, namely, for the Kingdom of God. To act for the sake of the Kingdom is to act for the sake of society.' (Pannenberg, *op.cit.*, p. 84).

The fact that we will never find the perfect political means and the ideal society does not invalidate our search for better ones. It rather makes it impossible for us to be satisfied with *any* existing society. The last thing a Christian can be is conservative; he has nothing to conserve. Any desire to preserve the past or the present as an ideal is a rejection of the Kingdom, which is in the future and is totally new. We do not seek change just for its own sake. But we know what the values of the Kingdom are and that they are political. We have to find the best means of realising them now, even though we are aware that they are provisional. To quote Pannenberg once again:

The new forms that are achieved will, in contrast with the ultimacy of God's Kingdom, turn out to be provisional and preliminary. They will in turn be called upon to give way to succeeding new forms.

Superficial minds might think that the political quest is therefore futile. They fail to recognize that the satisfaction is not in the perfection of that with which we begin but in the glory of that toward which we tend. We possess no perfect program, but are possessed by an inspiration that will not be realized perfectly by us. It is realized provisionally in the ever-renewed emergence of our striving in devotion to history's destiny. (*op.cit.*, pp. 80-1).

We prepare for the coming of the Kingdom by awakening faith in its coming. This we do not simply by trying to persuade people that what Christ said was true, but by giving them an experience of the Kingdom through our efforts to bring about peace, justice, and brotherhood. We will not convince people that the Kingdom is for real by arguing about scriptural texts. If we 'do the truth', the truth will speak for itself.

chapter 3
Love and Politics

Christianity is more concerned with what people do than with what they think, and there are doubtless many people who do the right thing for the wrong reasons. However, although theology is primarily concerned with reflecting on action, all Christian action is based on some, mostly prereflective or precritical, theology and it is necessary also to reflect upon and examine this and thus find motivation and inspiration for further action. Fortunately, most people do not need theological arguments to prove to them that Christianity has a lot to do with loving one's neighbour and, therefore, in South African society, with political action. The Gospel seems to them to be very clear on this. And it is; but only to those who have eyes to see and ears to hear. Most people see this, because most people are oppressed. But we, as Whites, have had our vision blurred and our hearing hardened by living in this society inescapably as part of the oppressing class and also by centuries of teaching, which, while claiming to be 'pure' Christianity, is based on and influenced by Western thought and Western cultural and social values.

The Churches generally agree that there is a need for 'social concern'. Many of them set up separate departments in their ecclesiastical structures to deal with it; which is an indication of their limited understanding of its nature. For some, such concern does not go beyond the running of soup kitchens and giving money to 'charity'; for others, it includes having a moral concern about certain aspects of society; for a few, it implies some political involvement. Whatever the extent of this concern, it is usually based on Christ's commandment to love our neighbour as ourselves and on such texts as 'By this shall all men know you are my disciples, if you have love for one another.' Love of neighbour is, therefore, seen in purely ethical terms, it is a moral obligation arising from Christ's express command and following from other parts of this teaching.

It would seem to be obvious that, even on this basis, an effective love of one's neighbour would require political action. However, many, probably the majority of White, Christians in South Africa do not recognise the direct connection between love and politics. Refuge from the political demands of the Gospel is sought in 'theological' and 'biblical' arguments, which are designed to prove that religion and politics do not mix.

Such arguments are really irrelevant, since, as we have seen, neither the Bible nor theology can provide us with ready-made answers to such questions. The Bible cannot tell us anything about politics as we understand them, because its authors simply did not understand them in that way. However, we will look at three of these arguments, basically on the terms of those who propose them, but noting some of the unquestioned presuppositions which underlie their appeal to the authority of the Bible.

One favourite argument is that religion and politics do not mix because each has its own distinctive sphere; the former is concerned with man's relationship with God and the latter with man's relationship with secular society. It is claimed that this argument is based on Christ's saying, 'Render to Caesar the things that are Caesar's and to God the things that are God's.' But is it?

The division of life into separate religious and political spheres was, historically, introduced for political reasons. The lack of a distinction between religion and politics led to the Church dominating the State. The politicians, therefore, were anxious to demarcate a separate sphere of activity for the Church. The theologians who supported this move were the radicals of their time and they welcomed the Church being rid of its secular privilege. The conservatives wanted the relationship to remain, because it was to their material advantage and what they considered to be the 'spiritual' interests of the Church: status, protection, financial support. They too could quote biblical texts: for example, '*All* authority in heaven and on earth is given to me.'

The politicians, however, won the day. Church and State were duly separated and this became accepted as the proper state of affairs. Most of us were born into a society where this separation was taken for granted. When, therefore, we read 'Render to Caesar' we tended to understand this as a confirmation of what we already believed. Clearly Christ's listeners did not understand it in this way, since they did not make any such distinction, and there is no biblical reason for us doing so. This, of course, is not meant to imply that we should seek to return to a Constantinian type of Church-State relationship. It is simply an illustration of how a theological rationalisation can be given to a political stance without any acknowledgement being given to its political origins.

Generally speaking, the argument that religion and politics do not mix is advanced by those who have a vested interest in keeping them

apart. This is why the distinction first arose and that is why it is
perpetuated. In South Africa the separation of religion from politics is
obviously used in the interests of the ruling party, but it also allows
others to enjoy the benefits of the system with an untroubled conscience.
The biblical command to love one's neighbour is acknowledged, but it
is left to the politicians to decide who our neighbour is and what the
limits of love are. The upholders of this argument may not mix religion
with politics, but they have allowed politicians to decide what
constitutes religion.

The Nationalist government has been allowed to give a very narrow
definition to 'religion' and a very broad one to 'politics'. I say 'allowed',
because many Church-people, not only members of the Dutch Reformed
Churches, are quite content, at least in practice, to accept the limits
that the government places on 'religion'. The government decides that
even personal relationships with people, for example, marriage or living
together in a community, are political matters. The Church then allows
its ministers to be appointed as government officials who implement the
government's laws on who may marry whom. It sets up separate
institutions for Black and White nuns or seminarians, it establishes
separate schools and hospitals. To refuse to do this would be considered
a 'political' action. To do it is clearly un-Christian. The Church,
however, has chosen to allow the government to remove certain
fundamental Christian duties from the religious sphere and to place
them in the political realm. Then, since many Church leaders share with
the Nationalists the view that religion and politics do not mix, it
restricts itself to an emasculated 'religion'. The Church, therefore, first
allows the government to draw the boundaries to its areas of concern
and then refuses to overstep these boundaries because that would be
'political'.

There are numerous other examples. Although such Gospel
injunctions as visiting the sick should not be taken as an exhaustive and
definitive description of a Christian's duty to his neighbour, they are
still clearly Christian things to do. The government, however, tells us
that, if the sick person happens to live in a Black area, we may not visit
him unless we obtain a permit. The Church bows its head, and its knee,
and asks for a permit; otherwise individuals feel excused from fulfilling
this Gospel injunction. To go without a permit would be considered a
'political' action, by both Church and State.

Let me give an example of this attitude from my own experience.
Before I was banned and house-arrested I had been participating in
worship with a group of friends in a private house. When I was banned I
unthinkingly followed the usual ecclesiastical practice and wrote to the
Minister of Justice asking permission to continue to do this. He refused,

but said that he would give me permission to attend 'a *bona fide* church'. It was then that I came to my senses and asked: what right has a politician to define what constitutes a church? I, therefore, decided that I would not ask for his permission and finally decided that I would simply go and would do so in as public a manner as possible, thus inviting prosecution. My church superiors could see absolutely no point in this action and could not understand why I did not simply ask for the permission that had been offered. To them the restriction of my rights was a 'political' matter; going to church was a 'religious' matter. They were thus applying the same definitions of 'religion' and 'politics' as the Minister had when he banned me in the first place. My refusal to accept the Minister's definition was to me an essentially religious matter, but the only way I could express this was by a political action, namely, by violating the terms of the restriction orders. Politically aware non-Christians, who were not in the least concerned whether I or anybody else ever went to church, could see at least the political significance of this. Those Christians who were blinded by their unquestioning acceptance of the government's claim to complete authority in what *it* defines to be 'political' could see no political or religious significance.

An added reason for Christians in South Africa being anxious to keep religion and politics apart is that the government has succeeded in making the word 'political' in certain contexts, a dirty word. A 'political' person is virtually synonymous with a 'subversive' person and, according to White, middle-class values, being subversive isn't nice. The almost inborn respect for 'law and order' has more to do with this argument than interpretation of the Bible does. The Bible is approached with this mentality, which cannot conceive of the Bible encouraging subversive activity. In a more normal society, the legitimacy of engaging in political activity as a means of loving one's neighbour might be more readily accepted. If one were concerned about housing needs, for example, one would not be expected to take the Bible literally and to shelter all the homeless in one's own home. But taking an active part in having someone elected to the local council or to parliament who would do something about it could also be seen as a Christian action. In South Africa, however, even drawing attention to such needs can be considered subversive. It is, therefore, convenient to be able to use the argument that religion and politics do not mix in order to avoid the unpleasant consequences that political involvement in South Africa tends to have.

We have seen in the previous chapter that Christianity and politics do and must mix. We do not have to search the Bible for a specific text to prove this. 'Only a cursory glance at the Bible is sufficient to establish two facts: that God is consistently represented as a political God and that he acts in history. To say that according to the biblical perspective,

God is a political being is to recognise that the various writers picture him in political terms . . . If politics is what God is doing, then equally politics is what people must do in response to God.' (J.G. Davies, *Christians, Politics and Violent Revolution,* pp. 11-12).

Christ's injunction to 'Render to Caesar the things that are Caesar's' does not contradict this. As Albert Nolan points out, in its context, this statement had nothing to do with the relationship between religion and politics; such a distinction would, in any event, have had no meaning for Jews of that time. 'For most Jews, paying tax to the Roman overlord meant giving to Caesar what belonged to God, namely, Israel's money and possessions. But for Jesus this was a rationalisation, a hypocritical excuse for avarice. It had nothing to do with the real issue.'*(op.cit.,* p. 95).

This argument, therefore, has no biblical justification and it carries very little weight in any modern society. It carries none at all in South Africa, where even the most obvious demands of loving one's neighbour are overridden by the dictates of a political ideology.

A second argument is that since Jesus himself did not engage in political activity, and in particular did not advocate the overthrow of the oppressive regime, neither should present-day Christians. Jesus did not fly in aeroplanes and he did not go to church. Are we to conclude, therefore, that the only acceptable mode of transport for a Christian is a donkey and that we should all attend the synagogue? We cannot read a twentieth-century understanding of 'political activity' into a first-century account of a person's life and teaching.

Jesus could only tell his listeners how they were to love in that particular society. We could hardly expect him to give us a Christian view on nuclear non-proliferation treaties. It does not matter, therefore, whether or not some of Christ's actions or teaching were 'political'. It cannot be argued from what he did in one situation to what he would have done in another one. He did not live in any other one. Our task is not to try to imagine what Christ would have done with the problems that we face. We simply do not know, because he did not in fact have to face them. (If we do want to indulge in such idle imaginings, I am sure that it would be easier to imagine Jesus taking part in a political demonstration than to imagine him behind the wheel of a Mercedes, or reclining in the back of a papal Cadillac.) In any case, the imitation of Christ is not to be interpreted as demanding reproduction of the details of Jesus' life. 'Jesus.' says F. Herzog, 'did not want Jesus copies. He expected each man to become free in his own freedom . . . Jesus alone had to take upon himself the cross to become the liberator. Discipleship is thus not doing over again what Jesus did. It is freely living *by what he did.*' (J.G. Davies, *op.cit.,* p.25).

It is generally agreed that Jesus was not a member of the armed revolutionary group of Zealots and he obviously did not have a detailed political policy or programme, as we understand them. In that sense we might be able to say that he was apolitical; but that is really not saying very much more than that he became man in the first century and not in the twentieth. As Gutierrez says: 'If we wished to discover in Jesus the least characteristic of a contemporary political militant we should not only misrepresent his life and witness and demonstrate a lack of understanding on our part of politics in the present world; we should also deprive ourselves of what his life and witness have that is deep and universal and, therefore, valid and concrete for today's man.' (*op.cit.*, p. 226).

Although Christ was concerned about the society of his time and indeed about every person whom he met, he was also interested in far more than that. His life and mission had dimensions which ours do not. He had to save the whole world. We do not. We are called to take up our cross, not his. Our mission in life follows from his and takes all its meaning from his, but we cannot claim to be doing all that he did and does. An active engagement in the narrow nationalistic politics of his time would have detracted from the universality of his mission. Whether or not Christ can be described as 'political' is not, therefore, the decisive question. The important question for the Christian is what the demands of Christ's teaching and practice are in our *present* historical situation. However, once this has been stated, we can go on to recognise that Christ's teaching and practice *did* have political implications in his own society.

Politics concern the relationships between people. To take the side of one group against another, as Christ did by identifying himself with the poor and condemning the rich, obviously has political implications. But, in the society in which Christ lived, the most delicate relationship was that between the Sadducees and the Romans. In the interests of religious freedom and the power and status which this brought them, the Sadducees had adopted a policy of peaceful co-existence with the Roman authorities. Christ did not directly disrupt this relationship. He was concerned about relationships between *all* people, not just this particular one. The Sadducees, however, were not slow in grasping the political implications of what Christ was saying and doing. They saw him as threatening their position of political compromise with the Romans. Why did they want him arrested and put to death? Because, 'if we leave him alone like this the whole populace will believe in him. Then *the Romans* will come and sweep away our temple *and our nation.*' (*Jn* 11.48). Why should the Romans have been concerned if Jesus was simply preaching a politically innocuous spiritual message? His message is only innocuous if it is spiritualised, privatised and domesticated for the benefit of the rich and the powerful.

Christ taught a new view of man which is a challenge to any political system, and a new understanding of authority which is a threat to any totalitarian system. The lording of power over others by those in authority - for example, by detaining people without trial or forcibly removing them from their homes - is clearly contrary to Christ's teaching. We do not have to find a particular biblical text that actually mentions detention or removals before we can condemn them as un-Christian. The lording of power is un-Christian but the form it takes in a particular time and place is politically determined and can only be opposed by political means.

That the Jews of Christ's time were oppressed by the Romans and that he did not incite his followers to overthrow them is not disputed. This, however, cannot be used as proof of Christ's apoliticism. It could rather be an example of his political realism. The Jews did not have the slightest chance of overthrowing the Romans - as was proved later. It would, therefore, have been politically naive and irresponsible for anyone to have encouraged them to try. There are, however, other and more subtle ways of being political. Is the Black Consciousness Movement, for example, not political because it does not call for a physical confrontation with the government? It is surely doing far more significant political work by helping people to rediscover their own identity, dignity and power.

There is a wealth of literature about the nature and extent of the political import of Christ's life and teaching and the implications of this for our own Christian practice. Obviously, not everybody can wade through it all and weigh up all the arguments. While such attempts to deepen and clarify our understanding of the Bible and its relevance to our own society are necessary, we do not have to be aware of them all in order to see that the acceptance of the Christian message today demands not only 'political charity' but also the radical questioning of *any* political system, and the rejection of any political ideology which seeks to impose its own total definition of man. All we really need to know is that Christ taught and showed that *God loves man.*

This is not a 'spiritual truth' proposed to us for our edification and contemplation. It is a fact that can only be realised by political action. We do not give our neighbour dignity by helping him or loving him; he has it because God loves him. If God loves him anything else about him is relatively unimportant. We cannot, therefore, accept anyone's right to decide that the most important thing about him is his race, class, achievement, or anything else. 'To preach the universality of love of the Father is inevitably to go against all injustice, privilege, oppression or narrow nationalism.' (Gutierrez, *op.cit.*, p. 232).

A third argument which is often used to justify a divorce between religion and politics maintans that Christianity is only concerned with the conversion of individuals and not with society. I am not concerned here with the false theological foundation of this argument, which is based on an 'individualist' understanding of salvation, but with the false anthropological and sociological presuppositions which underlie it. This argument implies a belief that society can be changed simply by changing individuals. It therefore presumes that one can deal with an individual without reference to the mutual relationships that exist between him and his society. But an individual does not and cannot exist in himself; he exists and only becomes a fully human person in interrelationship with other people, that is, in society. A person, therefore, can only change by changing his relationships with society; these are part of him. He cannot first become good in himself and then turn his attention to society, as if it were something completely removed from him. Changing oneself and changing society are not two separate actions; they are part of one and the same action.

All that this argument really says is that if we had a perfect political system, there would be no need for Christians to be politically involved; they could concern themselves with their personal moral failings that people would have in any society. Since we do not have a perfect political system a person can only *become* a better Christian by improving his relationship with society, because these enter into all of his actions. In South African society these cannot be improved without changing society itself. For a person to be a better Christian in terms of visiting the sick and imprisoned, for example, it would be necessary to secure the repeal of the 1913 and 1936 Land Acts, the Group Areas Act, the Internal Security Act, the Terrorism Act, and numerous other laws. That would seem to require some political action.

According to this argument it is possible for a Christian to ignore the evils of society and simply to get on with the job of being a good Christian in his private life. Its proponents might agree that conversion to Christianity implies some change in a person's private behaviour, for example, in his relationships with other individuals, and even perhaps in regard to how he votes. They would not, however, see a Christian's duty as extending to such public, political action as, for example, demonstrating in protest against the detention of people without trial. Our duty in this case, they would, and do, say, is to have a private word with the Minister of Justice or the Chief of the Security Police. But the detention of people is not due to some personal moral aberration of either of these gentlemen. It is a necessary means of maintaining the present structures of the society of which we are all part. Our attitude towards detention without trial is a reflection of our attitude to our society. We cannot, therefore, privately and individually condemn the society and yet support, even if only negatively by our silence, the public means of upholding it. We cannot be opposed simply as individuals and express our concern by sending a food parcel to a detainee (even if he/she would be allowed to receive it). We are not involved as individuals, but as members of a society. We can only express our disapproval of the public, political actions of that society by our own public, political action.

It is not possible to persuade the Minister of Justice that he would be a better Christian if he did not detain people without trial. He does not detain people because he is a Christian, but because he is a politician. He could only reject the principle of detention without trial if he first rejected the political and other presuppositions on which the whole Nationalist ideology is based, since this is what determines his understanding of Christianity. The false presuppositions lead to an un-Christian practice and the latter cannot be changed without the former being rejected. This is not to deny the power of the Christian message; it is simply taking account of the nature and limitations of its human agents.

Further, while we have a duty towards the perpetrators of injustice, our first duty is to the victims. We cannot leave them to their suffering while we exercise the greatest patience in trying to make those responsible see the light. It is no help or consolation to those who are dying of starvation or are languishing in jail to know that some people in the privacy of their conscience strongly disapprove of such injustice. All the time spent in trying quietly to persuade the oppressor to change his mind without upsetting him by making too many demands is, in the eyes of the oppressed, time spent in being party to their oppression. In the South African situation, this argument may be countered on a pragmatic level by pointing out that this approach has been tried for a very long time. There is no sign of it succeeding and we do not have time to go on trying.

Finally, 'the view that by changing people you will ultimately change society is', as J.G. Davies points out, 'much too facile'. He argues: 'A good person is hard to find in an unjust society which itself hinders people from loving others and seduces them into attitudes of dominance and violence. Moreover those whose goodwill has been cultivated exclusively within personal relationships are frequently blind to social injustice and to the sufferings of those they do not meet.' (*op.cit.*, p. 17).

There are many Christians in South Africa, both clerical and lay, who steadfastly hold to some or all of the arguments we have discussed and who sincerely believe that the only good Christian is an apolitical one. I do not dispute the sincerity of their views, but only their right to claim a theological and biblical foundation for them. But there are others, and these are the ones I am primarily addressing, who, with at least equal sincerity, believe that loving one's neighbour necessarily entails political action. Even these, however, usually stop short of radical political action.

There are, I believe, a number of reasons for this. One is, as we have seen, the idealist nature of their basic understanding of Christianity. Another is the distinction which is made between loving God as a religious activity and loving one's neighbour as an ethical duty. They agree that loving one's neighbour is important, but loving God comes first. 'Loving God', in this context, usually seems to mean some purely spiritual activity which is expressed by religious actions. As such it is quite impossible for man to do and so there is no question of it coming first. Much as he might like to, and much as he may even convince himself that he does, man cannot indulge in the exercise of loving God as a separate religious activity. If he could, he would not be man, he would be a spirit, and the recipient would not be the Christian God; he would be a god cut down to the size of the other objects of our love. This is simply a little more polite way of saying what St John says quite bluntly: 'Anyone who says "I love God" and hates his brother is a liar.'

We can say the words 'I love God' and sincerely believe that we mean them, but we are giving quasi-magical power to words. Statements do not become true because of the depth of feeling with which we say them. They must be true in fact. The statement 'I love God' can only be true if it is made by a person who actually does love God by loving his neighbour. St John continues: 'the man who does not love the brother whom he can see cannot love God whom he has never seen'. He does not say that such a person *does not* love God but that he *cannot*. He cannot because, as Schillebeeckx says, 'the Christian loves his fellow man with the same love with which he loves God and with the same love with which he and his fellow man are loved by God' (*God and Man*, p. 203).

With the incarnation, Christianity became a human religion; a human response to a divine initiative. However, from the time of the birth of monasticism, concerted attempts have been made to 'spiritualise' it. A 'spiritualised' religion is, of course, far easier to deal with. It overcomes most problems by declaring them to be irrelevant because they are concerned with the body or the world and, something which was particularly important at a later stage, it does not get you into trouble with the secular authorities or disturb your compromise with them. One of the reasons for this tendency was the acceptance of the Platonic distinction between body and soul, with the soul being all that really mattered. Assuming the soul to be superior, God, despite all that He said and did in the Bible, was presumed to be more interested in it than in the body. While the philosophical origins of this approach become obscured and not consciously referred to, its influence persisted. Thus, for example, when Christ speaks of setting prisoners free and liberating the oppressed, the message was interpreted 'spiritually' to mean 'those who are prisoners to their own self-will' or 'those who are oppressed by their sins'. It could not actually refer to those locked in jail or who were physically oppressed. Those things concern only the body in which God is presumed not to be really interested. This is clearly a very comforting and comfortable interpretation for those who are doing the physical oppression or at least benefiting from it. It is not simply coincidence that such interpretations were first made by people who, in virtue of their status as clerics, were themselves part of the oppressive class.

Most theologians would now reject such purely 'spiritual' interpretations, but this is not true of popular preaching. Christ actually gave sight to the physically blind, but Roman Catholics for example are only concerned with 'sight to the inly blind' (*People's Hymnbook,* No. 128). Very rarely, if ever, will one hear a priest or a minister tell a congregation of rich White South Africans that having two or three motor cars and an income of R20,000, R30,000 or even more a year makes it very difficult for them to enter the Kingdom of Heaven. No, it will be explained, Christ did not condemn riches as such; it is our attitude to them that is important. If there were no oppressed people and if everybody were rich, it might be legitimate to interpret the Gospel in this 'spiritual' way, but it cannot be valid in a world where the few are rich not only in comparison with but at the expense of the majority who are poor.

The implicit acceptance of the distinction between body and soul reinforces the separation of love of God from the love of man. Since the soul is considered to be the higher part of man, it is taken for granted that when we are dealing with such a sublime concept as the love of God this must be seen as pertaining to the soul. Neil Middleton has pointed out that when the classical 'spiritual' authors write about the love of God, they almost invariably talk about 'souls' and not about people. (cf. *The Language of Christian Revolution,* pp. 97-104). The problem with this approach, which can be very appealing emotionally to people's religious sentiments, is that 'souls' do not exist. People do. If I am going to relate to or respond to God, I can only do so as a human person, because that is what I am. And this, as we have already seen, necessarily includes my social relationships. I cannot relate to God without these social relationships, because then it would not be 'I' that was doing the relating. If God had wanted a purely spiritual response He would not have made man the complex and social creature that he is; neither would there have been any reason for His son to become man.

But, it might be asked, do we not have a direct relationship with God through the work of the Holy Spirit? We do, and, on God's part, it is a direct spiritual relationship, but we, not being God, can only know, express, and respond to this relationship in a human way; otherwise it would not be 'we' who were responding. We receive the Holy Spirit; we do not become Him. We only have knowledge of this relationship because we believe that God has revealed it to us. But 'when God speaks, He does so ultimately in order to be heard by man; and for this reason His spoken revelation cannot possibly reach our conscious inwardness in a purely internal, vertical manner' (Schillebeeckx, *God and Man,* p. 190).

God made us, deals with us, and saves us *as men.* We must, therefore, respond as men. 'It is our grace to be fully men, sharing in the "humanity" of God, which is simply to be man in a divine way; to remain in vital contact with the well-spring of our being as we meet our fellows and fulfil our task in the world; to be permeated by a divine dynamism. However we try to express this perpetual and all-embracing presence of the divine, however faltering and stammering our words, it effects in us a relationship to God which is intensely existential, personal and personalising, and which *is truly realised* in the "sacrament" of love for the world and for men.' (Frahsen, *op.cit.,* vol.I, p. 94; my italics). There is no point in following Bernard of Clairvaux's example and envying the angels (cf. Middleton, *op.cit.,* p. 95). We are not angels and it is neither possible nor virtuous to try to act as if we were.

The relationship we have with God is certainly one of love, but, as St John says, 'The love I speak of is not our love for God, but the love He showed for us in sending his Son' (*1 Jn* 4.10). In the New Testament, 'love of God' almost invariably refers to something we *have* and not to something we *do.* What we *do* is love our neighbour and thus also love God, because the love with which we are loving is the love we have received from Him, which is the love with which He loves everybody. God, by giving us a share in His love, has not only made it possible for us to love Him by loving our neighbour. He has also made it impossible for us to love Him without loving our neighbour. It is impossible not simply because to fail to love our neighbour is to break His commandment and thus to displease Him. It is impossible because when I love my neighbour it is no longer I alone who am doing so. I am loving with the love He has given me and, therefore, since 'God is love', together with Him.

I also love Him with this same love. Either I have this love or I do not. I cannot have it in respect of God and at the same time not in *respect* of my neighbour, because it is the same love. Since I am human, the only way I can know whether I do or do not have this love is by looking at my relationship with my neighbour. If I am loving my neighbour then I know that I am also loving God, because 'God himself dwells in us if we love one another' (*Jn* 4.12). There can be no question, therefore as to which comes first, loving God or loving one's neighbour. It is the same love, God's love, in both cases and we either have it in relation to both or not at all.

The important thing for the mystic and the political activist alike is that God first loved us. And, as St Augustine says, 'because He has loved me, he has made me lovable' - that is, able to love and able to be loved. We do not love God in return for His love; we simply return His love by loving our neighbour.

It cannot be concluded from Christ's saying that the first commandment is to love God and the second is to love our neighbour, that he was giving an order of priority or implying any separation between the two. They were stated separately in the Old Testament and Christ's point was that these two, which are in fact one, constitute the great commandment which is more important than all the thousands of other legal prescriptions found in the Old Testament put together. He himself said that his 'new commandment' was 'love one another as I have loved you' and the mark of his disciples was to be their love for one another, not any esoteric religious practice. For St Paul, too, all the commandments are summed up in 'this *single* commandment: you must love your neighbour as yourself' (*Rom*. 13.9). We love God in our fellow men and we love our fellow man in God.

Love of man and of the world is, therefore, an expression of our love of God; it is the exercise of the love which God has given us. It is not the *only* expression of this love; but it *is* the only expression that can be known and measured and is thus the only way of testing the validity and authenticity of other expressions. Praising, thanking, adoring God in worship are also expressions of love. But we cannot leave aside our social relationships even when we worship and acts of worship are meaningless if these relationships are not loving ones.

This is, of course, a humanising of the Gospel, but it is God who is responsible for such humanising. It was He who decided to reveal his love by becoming man. We meet God primarily in Christ: in the Bible, in the sacraments, in our fellow man and in the world. In meeting him we meet God directly, but the test which he himself set for our commitment to him was 'whatever you do to any of these the least of my little ones'. Difficult though it may be in practice, we can also meet God in the Church. Our response to these meetings, however, cannot be separated from our response to the meeting in our neighbour and we cannot use them as an escape from, or substitute for, our commitment to our neighbour.

Any response can only be made in and with the love that God shares with us; and it can only be made by us, that is, by real human people, not 'souls'. If we do not have the love of God in us, which according to St John we do not if we do not love our brothers, there is simply no way in which we can meet or love God, no matter what intensity of 'religious' feeling we might build up in relation to the Christ of the Gospels, or of the sacraments, or to some idea of 'god'. Such feelings would be *our* feelings whereas our love of God would be *His* love in us. Once again, it is neither our love for God nor our love for our neighbour which comes first. Both are the expression of the love which God has for us. But the only one that can be measured and the one by which all claims to loving God are measured is, as St John, particularly, makes clear, our love of our neighbour. It might seem that John contradicts this when he goes on to say that if we love God we will also love his children. But he is simply stressing the oneness of the love; he does not say that loving our brother *follows* from our loving God.

Those who insist on the primacy of the love of God may be trying to safeguard the recognition of the importance of God. In fact, however, they are in more danger of minimising God's role than are those who emphasise love of neighbour. In separating the two they make love of neighbour a purely human activity which man indulges in in response to God's love for him; they thus restrict the effectiveness of God's salvation and limit his love. (There is also the danger that the primary concern becomes *my* love of God rather than my love of *God.*) They turn man into something like a spiritual coca-cola machine: you must keep putting something in one end so that something else comes out the other. If you neglect to put something in, you dry up. But if you are sharing in an infinite love and it is this love you are exercising when you love your neighbour, you cannot use it up. We do not love God so that we may have the strength to love others. We do not charge ourselves up with spiritual energy and then expend it on 'wordly' activity and then go back for a recharge.

Another consequence of separating love of God from love of neighbour is that the neighbour is treated simply as an object on which we exercise our charity. He is not treated as a person, but as a means to our growth in the love of God. He is not loved for himself, but 'for the sake of God'. It is not, however, possible to love someone for the sake of somebody else, even God. You can be kind to him, treat his wounds, educate him, feed him; but you cannot love him. I sometimes think that one of the reasons for 'religious' people being frightened of radical political change is that they fear that if it occurred they would not have any opportunity for practising their charity.

If one is concerned about the whole man one cannot avoid politics; they are essential to his being, or to his being deprived of being, a man. The institutional church, however, in its undoubtedly sincere zeal for charitable work, tries to stand aloof from politics. As long as the priests and nuns can do their work, politics can be left to the politicians. The result of this attitude is that the priests deal with 'souls' and the nuns with 'sickness' or 'education'; neither group is concerned with people.

While such means of expressing love of one's neighbour as caring for the sick or teaching might not be overtly political, they do, particularly in South Africa, have political implications. A doctor cannot say that he is only interested in the sick and that politics are no concern of his. He has political obligations both as a person and specifically as a doctor. If, for example, he works in a mission hospital, he cannot help seeing that the sickness of probably the majority of his patients is directly attributable to political causes: lack of land and migratory labour. If thousands of people are to be moved by government decree into an area which is incapable of supporting them, where malnutrition is already rife and where the medical facilities are inadequate, does not a doctor, as a doctor, have a duty to use all means, including political ones, to prevent this? What does a doctor do when he is told that for political reasons he must not diagnose so many cases of T.B., or that starvation does not officially exist so he must not give it as a cause of death? (As happened at a mission hospital in the Northern Cape.)

If we see the love of our fellow man simply in terms of fulfilling a commandment or as following from our love of God, we will not appreciate its central place in Christian life. In the former case, our response is liable to be minimal - doing just enough to avoid breaking a commandment; in the latter, it will be very secondary. While we may thus be led to some political action, it is not likely to be wholehearted and radical; it may be seen as just one of the many moral obligations that Christians have. But the love of neighbour we have been discussing here is not primarily a matter of ethics; it is not enough to see it even as the greatest ethical demand. This love derives its meaning from God's saving work and is our means of participating in that work; 'it is essentially a *religious* event, a religious task, and not simply "morality" ' (Schillebeeckx, *God and Man,* p. 222). The Church in South Africa does not seem to go beyond seeing it as 'morality'; hence its political action consists in little more than moralising. The Church does have the duty to 'moralise', to criticise, and it would have this in any society, since there can never be a perfect society. In the South African situation this is clearly not enough. The Church, however, is unlikely to move beyond this if the only motivation for its action is the fulfilment of a commandment to love one's neighbour.

All this is not to say that the political activist who is working for the creation of a better society has necessarily 'fulfilled the Law' and that he can rest assured that he is a better Christian than his apolitical brother. Love of neighbour only has the meaning and importance given to it here if it is a genuine, disinterested love. The activist can be just as concerned about himself as the pietist may be; whereas the latter may be primarily concerned with his own holiness and his personal salvation, the former may be primarily concerned with his own reputation or desire for power. Although it is true that 'Greater love no man has than he lays down his life for his friend', St Paul warns that it is possible even to give oneself to be burnt at the stake and yet not to have love.

There is, however, no danger that if we love our brother too much we will have nothing left for God. If we are really loving our brother we are *thereby* loving God.

What distinguishes the Christian from the humanist is not the sort of actions which they perform, but the Christian's belief that God has given an added meaning to such actions. Because he believes this he will also have the desire and the need to turn to God; not to seek a respite from his activity nor to have a recharge, but simply because He is there. It is not necessary to bring God in; He has come in. As Christians, no matter how active we are, we need to keep the awareness of this alive. In practice there may be a lack of this awareness, but this does not arise from the nature of our activity. It probably derives rather from a reaction to the forms and language in which such awareness is usually expressed. The old ecclesiastical 'god-talk' is not made relevant to modern man simply by being set to guitar music. That, however, is another question, which we cannot go into here.

I have discussed the relationship between loving God and loving one's neighbour at some length because I think it is important to show that an emphasis on the political expression of one's love of one's neighbour is not an expression of the 'demented activism', of which some of the more 'pious' Christians accuse their more politically-minded brethren; nor does it imply equating Christianity with humanism. I have not suggested that the sum total of the Christian message is: get involved in political action. But I do most strongly suggest that as the Church in South Africa, where people are deliberately dehumanised as a direct result of the implementation of a political ideology, our emphasis must be on loving God by and in loving our neighbour not only on a personal level but also by direct political action. In less evil circumstances people might emphasise other expressions of their love of God; though never to the exclusion of the love of others, which remains the *only* means of measuring and testing the validity of this love. We are not, however, concerned with other times and places. Christianity is not a matter of abstract, academic arguments or opinions; it demands an active response here and now. In South Africa, political action is not something for which the need might arise; the need is there all the time.

chapter 4
Religious Schizophrenia

On the basis of an 'idealist' understanding of 'Christian truth', the
Church has tried to turn Christianity into a self-contained religious
system, with a fixed set of beliefs and a code of behaviour which
follows from these. People are called Christians if they believe these
truths; they are good Christians if they live up to these beliefs by
observing the moral laws. But there is no direct connection between
what they believe and what they do; believing is seen as a separate
intellectual activity. It is possible therefore to believe but not to live up
to this belief; this is simply a moral fault. It follows from the fact that
you accept certain truths that you *should* behave in a certain way, but
if you do not behave in this way you are still a Christian, because you
still believe. This is religious schizophrenia.

The only 'treatment' that the Church offers such people is the
encouragement to be more faithful to the truths in which they profess
to believe. Since these truths are considered to be objective and free
from the influence of social and political factors, such exhortation also
tries to be free from these. The whole exercise, therefore, has an air of
unreality about it. It is unreal because it is divorced from the real
world of politics, social relationships, class struggle and history.

This unreal, spiritualised, and essentially private character which the
Church has given to Christianity is attractive to many people, primarily
because, by producing a spiritual answer to very physical problems, it
saves one from really having to come to grips with these problems. This
is very comfortable for the rich - which was the object of the exercise in
the first place - because it means that such matters as how much money
they have and how they make it have little to do with their Christianity.
Provided that they do not make it in some obviously 'immoral' way,
such as by running brothels, and provided they give alms to 'the
deserving poor', the Church has nothing to say to them except to
encourage them to practise 'spiritual detachment' from their wealth.

The docility which is instilled in the poor by such an approach is also
of great advantage to the rich, since such 'Christianity' helps to defuse
any threat to their wealth and power. But it also has an appeal to the

poor and oppressed themselves in that it provides an answer, albeit a false one, to a very real need: the need to be released from the dreary, suffering, soul-destroying world of oppression and exploitation. 'Christianity', however, has been, and still is to a great extent, used to offer a release by providing an escape. Even an escape into an unreal world can be welcomed by people who see no possibility of true release from their condition. Thus people who spend their lives in shacks and hovels can sing with great fervour of heavenly mansions, crystal seas, and celestial banquets; at least for an hour or two they can live in a better world.

There is, of course, an element ot truth in such an approach, but it also debases Christian hope into a mere dream of heaven. While such dreaming may help some people to come to terms with their position, it can offer nothing to the ever-increasing number of people who have no desire to come to terms with an oppressive situation, but want to change it.

It is possible that in other times and places, for very practical reasons, there might have been nothing else that people could have done other than come to terms with an unsatisfactory situation: it might have been simply technologically or economically impossible. In the modern world, however, the means for changing an unjust society are available, though choosing the right ones and gaining access to them may be a complex and lengthy process. But answers which might have been valid in different circumstances cannot automatically be taken as valid now. (It is not only Church people who make the mistake of thinking that if something was once true it must always be so. Thus some members of the Liberal Party seem to think that if one says that the policy of the Liberal Party as formulated in the 1950s does not meet the needs of South Africa in the 1970s one thereby rejects the role that they played 20-odd years ago. Their type of multiracialism might have been the right approach then, but it does not follow that it is now.)

Man needs answers to the questions which life in any society raises; he needs to give some meaning to his world. The answers and meaning which Christianity gave in the past may have met the needs of those times and so have been valid. But they do not remain valid forever. And this not because Christianity changes, but because man and his world change and Christianity is the response of man in and of a particular world to the God historically revealed and historically responded to in the Bible.

Because the Christian response is an historical one, the response of the Church in other ages is not really relevant to a discussion of the *present* role of the Church. It is not possible for us, with our understanding both of the Bible and of society, to pass judgement on the morality of actions performed by people with a fundamentally different understanding of these. The rightness of the Church's approach, therefore, cannot be argued from the glories of its past successes: the billions of followers it has gained over the past two thousand years; the numerous outstanding figures it has produced; the great service it has rendered humanity in the fields of education, medicine, the arts, etc. There is also a negative side to the history of the Church but, in any event, I do not wish to deny its past achievements. All I am saying is that, on the basis of an idealist approach, it cannot effectively meet the needs of modern man.

It is true that even today this approach can, and does, motivate people to be concerned about the evils of political systems and to work actively for their improvement. Does the precise nature and motivation of their commitment really matter, provided they are trying to overcome suffering and injustice? I think it does, because the 'idealist' approach leads many very concerned people to expend a great deal of time and energy in looking for the right answer to the wrong question. The question is not how do we put our Christianity into practice in this situation, but what *is* Christianity in this situation.

The first question assumes that 'our Christianity' contains the answer and so begs the basic question. The only answer it can give lies in the prescription of a cure without a diagnosis. If the patient continues to ail, the dosage is increased; which does not really help when the diagnosis is wrong. The Church in South Africa has in the past verbally condemned apartheid and has encouraged a certain degree of multiracialism. As the situation deteriorates it issues more and more condemnation, calls for more and more multiracial meetings, more and more education to change people's attitudes, in the belief that this is the Christian remedy. It does not question whether the obvious failure of this remedy might be due not to the amount of the dosage, but to the fact that the prescription is wrong, because it is based on a false diagnosis. Such a remedy may be applied with the greatest dedication and it may even alleviate some of the symptoms of the disease, but it can never cure it.

Our faith, because of its and our nature, must interact with society. The different denominational churches in South Africa are, in varying degrees, becoming increasingly aware of this. But they are fighting a losing battle, because of their insistence that the interaction must take place on their terms. They are trying to deal with people on the basis of their preconceived idea of what they should be, rather than with people as they in fact are. (It is the preconceived nature of the idea of what they should be that I am objecting to, not the attempts to make people better.) We, as Christians, do not know what people should be; we only know that they should, and can, be better. What the 'better' is and how to achieve it are part of the problem. The Church, however, assumes that all that is needed is that people become good Christians, according to *its* understanding of what makes a good Christian. In answer to the question, 'How does one become a good Christian today, in the present unjust South African situation?' it replies, 'Be a good Christian'. Any more specific advice which follows from this general injunction still assumes that there is a simple Christian answer to every problem. Such advice cannot lead to *inter*action with society; the most it can lead to is action by Christians on society.

It is not only the language in which this advice is so often couched that makes it sound foreign and irrelevant to the world, but also the base from which it is given. Christianity does have a special contribution to make, but it does not make it *to* the world from outside. The Church does not only have a role as 'the conscience of society'; it is also part of that society. Christ himself emphasised his role as servant rather than as judge; the Church, however, tends to reverse the emphasis. The Church does have the right to criticise, but it should also heed Bob Dylan's advice: 'Don't criticise what you can't understand'. If the Church is to serve, or even to criticise, it must listen. This is not an attempt to water down the demands of Christianity in order to make it acceptable to the world. It is an accommodation only in the sense that Christ accommodated himself to the same world by becoming man. We do not have to apologise for the meaning and motivation that Christianity gives to our political involvement, but neither must we be so complacent and superior about it that we believe that only Christians can root out the evils of our society. For the Church to be a Christian Church, it must take seriously not only the problems of the world but also the solutions which are offered from outside the Church. 'She must allow herself to be guided by the autonomous laws of this world's structures and tasks.' (Schillebeeckx, *God the Future of Man,* p. 135). This is not something that must be done in addition to, or as a consequence of, Christian teaching: it is essential to the Christianness of any response.

Some people might still be satisfied with a Christianity which affords them spiritual consolation in their trials and sufferings and promises them a reward in the hereafter; and which thus enables them to escape from or ignore all worldly problems. This would be all very well if man lived in isolation and if Christianity were only concerned with the individual and not with all men and the transformation of the whole world. Whether we like it or not, man, more so in modern society than in previous ones, does not live in isolation. His personal beliefs are not only his concern; they influence his relationships not only with other people but also with the social and political institutions of society.

In South African society virtually every action one performs, from the way one greets a person to the way one votes, has political overtones and we cannot escape from this by claiming to be concerned only with God and with our personal relationships with others. Such a 'religion' in its attitude to political problems only excludes the possibility of solving them, and this too is a political action. This religion is basically a produce of the middle class and is tied to their individualistic 'liberal' politics, but since they have dominated the Church by their power, wealth and education it has been foisted by them onto the poor as Christianity. But it can only be considered 'Good News' by those poor who have resigned themselves to their present position, whereas Christianity gives hope for liberation *now*, not in some, timeless, unknown future.

It is true that a 'simple faith' has inspired and enabled many people to lead very good lives and to be genuinely concerned about their neighbour on both the personal and the political level. Such people are usually found among the poor. This, I believe, is no accident, but is due to the genuineness of the gut-level feelings and responses of poor people which survive the middle-class Church's attempt to rationalise and spiritualise their position. This does, however, tend to lead to a separation of religion - since this is defined by the Church - and socio-political action, and hence to religious schizophrenia.

It is not the lack of intellectual content which is the reason for rejecting this 'simple faith', but the false intellectual content which has been given to it by the teaching Church. I would certainly not suggest that it is necessary to be intellectual or educated in order to be a Christian. But, in order to allow and to encourage people to respond in their own way, it is necessary to expose the false assumptions which form the basis of a theory which justifies a simple and essentially otherwordly faith.

Once this has been done, Christianity can be presented as basically a simple message, particularly for those with whom the Gospel is primarily concerned: the poor and the oppressed. Sometimes it will be as simple as saying, 'Right on'. In other words, the meaning of the message will be determined to a great extent by the efforts of the poor and oppressed as they struggle to liberate themselves, instead of it being taught *to* them in a foreign language. However, no matter how simple the message may be, it still has to be made true in an increasingly complex world.

Christianity does not provide an escape from the present either in the contemplation of the past or in dreaming of the future. It is a present hope that the past can be realised and the future anticipated in the present. We do not simply set this hope over against the present. We have to realise this hope in the present.

We cannot do this by saying, 'We don't believe in Apartheid, we hope in the Gospel'. The Gospel is not an ideology which we hold in contradiction to the ideology of apartheid, as is implied for example in a statement issued by the South African Council of Churches after its offices had been raided by the Security Police: 'We do advocate a social order fundamentally different from the present apartheid set-up in South Africa and we do so on the grounds of our understanding of the Gospel of Jesus Christ. Over against Apartheid, which proclaims the immutable separation of people, the Gospel, we believe, proclaims the unity of mankind.' (*Ecunews Bulletin, 38,* 1976, p. 4). Earlier in the statement, it was said: 'We are party to no plots and plans', thus suggesting that belief in the Gospel makes all plotting and planning unnecessary. But our *belief* (in the sense of an intellectual assent which is clearly the meaning here) that the Gospel proclaims the unity of mankind does nothing to make it happen. To make this belief true, it might well be necessary in certain circumstances to plot and plan. (Was Bonhoeffer being un-Christian by his plotting? Does the smuggling of Bibles into communist countries not involve plotting and planning?)

The advocating of a fundamentally different society must certainly be done on the grounds of our understanding of the Gospel, but if it is to be more than wishful thinking it must be given practical effect, which in a totalitarian state would almost inevitably involve action which could be termed 'plotting'. At the very least, it cannot be assumed, as the Council appears to do, that plotting and planning cannot be demands of the Gospel.

It is possible, of course, that this assumption is based more on the fear of the Terrorism Act than on an understanding of the Gospel. Is it perhaps assumed that Christianity could not possibly demand the performance of an action which might carry the death penalty or a sentence of life imprisonment? I would have thought that there were quite a lot of precedents for Christians suffering such a fate. Or is there perhaps a further assumption that it is only pagans who kill Christians and that in a Christian country like South Africa it is only communists who go to jail? (All such assumptions are, of course, White ones. While there are few, if any, White Christians among long-term political prisoners, there are Black ones.)

The Gospel is subversive of all evil and the evil of apartheid does not lie simply in men's minds. To subvert that evil it is not enough to proclaim a *belief* in something else. Proclaiming abstract beliefs is a fairly safe pastime even in South Africa; it is also a fairly irrelevant one. But it is the only one that the Church can indulge in if it continues only to talk to the world from its idealist haven.

Something of the idealist approach is seen even in those more progressive Christians who talk in terms of 'living beyond the crisis' or 'establishing liberated zones'. This approach suggests that since Christian truth cannot be applied in the present real situation an attempt should be made to apply it to an unreal one. But Christian truth is not to be *applied* in any situation; we have to 'do the truth' and make the truth in a particular historical time and place. While this is done in the light of the future, we cannot know what the Christian response in a future historical situation would be; this response can only be worked out in the present.

It is our hope in the future that makes us radically dissatisfied with the present but it is not an expression of hope to ignore our present society or to seek to escape from it into one of our own making. The future orientation of this approach contains an element of truth, but there is also a very real danger, of which Gutierrez warns: 'One must be very careful not to replace a Christianity of the Beyond with a Christianity of the Future, if the former tends to forget the world, the latter runs the risk of neglecting a miserable and unjust present and the struggle for liberation.' (*op.cit.*, p. 218). The new society must arise out of the present one. Our present one is the result of a complex and ruthlessly enforced political ideology, which cannot simply be ignored or wished away. While we should try to live according to the values of the future, our main concern is how to give these meaning in our *present* society. 'The new reality comes not so much from projecting ideal programs, but more from identifying social forces at work in a situation that have the promise of enabling us to transcend what is unjust about the present order . . . We must find ways of sustaining and supporting and of being part of critical struggles within our society. Without this kind of concrete historical form, the ultimate religious hope becomes empty; it becomes a deceit, it becomes something which people concerned about the well-being of their fellows must condemn.' (T.W. Ogletree, in *From Hope to Liberation,* ed. N. Piediscalzi, pp. 46-7).

The failure to see Christianity as a present, historically conditioned response to the Gospel empties even the more specifically religious actions of the Church of content. We cannot leave our historical conditions out of account even in our acts of worship. Christ was not simply giving a moral command when he said, 'If, when you are bringing your gift to the altar, you suddenly remember that your brother has a grievance against you, leave your gift where it is before the altar. First go and make your peace with your brother, and only then come back and offer your gift.' (*Mt* 5.23/4). The prophets who condemned the sacrifices of those who were unjust in their dealings with their fellow men as empty offerings, despised by God, were not just moralising. They were saying that worship and injustice are incompatible.

The unjust person *cannot* worship; he cannot have a religious attitude to God separate from his attitude to his fellow man. We cannot,

therefore, draw the strength from worship to behave better towards
others. Our relationships with others are part of our worshipping self;
if these are unjust, our worship can be no more than lip service. We
cannot lay aside our social relationships for the hour or two that we
worship, with the hope that we may return to them in a better frame of
mind. The social context is as much part of our worship as it is of our
faith. Yet how many times do we hear, in South African churches,
sermons that could have been preached 30 or 40 years ago in London or
Dublin? We are not addressed as people, but as a collection of
disembodied 'hearts and minds', which are 'to be raised up to God'. The
'truths' which are preached have been preserved in a spiritual hot-house
and are presented to us, or rather to our hearts and minds, in the
rarefied atmosphere of the church building. Any influence they may
have on our social and political lives is, and can only be, secondary; the
important thing is that we acknowledge with our minds the rightness of
the truth. This might have some practical implications, but they are
only implications and usually apply only on the personal level. They are
things that we must do in addition to, or as a consequence of,
worshipping; they are not part of the one act of worship. But we cannot
'offer ourselves to God', as we are exhorted to do, if our selves are
entangled in an unjust social system. We may imagine that we can and
so become schizophrenic, which is the logical consequence of such
religion.

It is this schizophrenic religion, which results from applying abstract
'truths' to 'hearts and minds', that enables people, with complete good
faith, to take part in the Eucharist before setting off to drop napalm on
innocent people; or, less dramatically, to leave 'the girl' at home
preparing the breakfast while they go to church in their Mercedes or
Jaguar. I am referring to something far more fundamental and far-
reaching than the usual criticism of 'Sunday Christians'. What I am
saying is that even if all Christians did all that is presently asked of
them by the Church, it would make very little difference to the unjust
political situation in South Africa, because the 'truth' which the Church
is preaching belongs to another world and the moral obligations that
are deduced from it are basically apolitical and ahistorical, and they
cannot be otherwise.

Man, whether considered as a politician or as a Christian, is not a
purely intellectual being; he is also governed by many other forces; His
political practice or social behaviour, therefore, cannot be changed
simply by changing his mind. As John Davies says, 'An idea which can
be shifted by argument is only an opinion, it is not a belief arising out
of a person's real being; and the shifting of such an opinion is not going
to change the person. People's real beliefs are derived from deep social

experience, as Marx saw so clearly, and the way to change people is to face them with a new social experience. We only increase guilt if we demand from people behaviour for which, due to their social experience, they have no capacity.' (J.D. Davies, *op.cit.*, p. 222).

People's opinions, even their theological ones, about apartheid are not the problem; their practice of it is. Apartheid is not an abstract theory that can be dispassionately debated. It is a very real practice in which everybody in South Africa is caught up. It is their experience of the 'benefits' of apartheid that leads Whites to support it, and the experience of the costs of these 'benefits' that leads Blacks to reject it. Changing the opinions of Whites might improve their personal relationships with a few individual Blacks, but it will not lead them to change the political and social structures that are the cause of the oppression of Blacks.

chapter 5
The Need for a Political Option

In its attempt to give 'religious' answers to political problems, the Church in fact legitimises a *reformist* political approach. No effort is made to *prove* that a reformist approach is the best one; it is *assumed* to be the one for Christians because this is what Christians have tended to do in other times and places.

Because the actual social and historical conditions of man are not treated as an integral part of any Christian response, such a response cannot be a true response to a historical situation; it can only be a legitimisation of the presuppositions on which their understanding of Christianity is based. In the case of the Church in South Africa, these presuppositions include the assumption of a Western way of thought and of middle-class, capitalist values. Since the Church does not acknowledge this, but claims to be preaching Christianity pure and simple, any action which it proposes can only be within a Western, middle-class, capitalist framework. This framework has become part of its 'pure' Christianity.

It cannot be claimed that the Church is above such considerations as the taking of a reformist or revolutionary political stance. The Church is inescapably part of society, both because its members are social beings and because it is a social institution. Simply by being present in a society it affects and is affected by that society. It cannot, therefore, avoid being involved with the politics of that society. The Church owns land, pays taxes, establishes institutions in areas which are reserved for one population group, has its ministry to the imprisoned curtailed by Security Laws, etc. All these, which are part of the Church's life in our society, are political considerations. It does not help to say: 'We are doing our best within the system,' when it is the system itself that is the problem; to say that is, in any event, to take a political stance - a *reformist* one.

Secondly, and more importantly, the Church cannot stand aside from politics, because politics are an essential and inseparable part of the

Christianness of the response of historical man to the historical biblical events. As we have seen, this is more in keeping with the biblical understanding of man's response to God's actions than is the basically hellenistic understanding which is assumed in the Church's present practice. The refusal to recognise this is to assume, even in one's actions as a Christian, the validity of the values of the *status quo.*

The Church in South Africa, in its attempts to be as apolitical as possible, succeeds only in being politically naive. In limiting itself to those aspects of particular problems which it considers to be of direct Christian concern and trying to ignore the political aspects, it limits itself to treating the symptoms and ignores the causes. Its actions are thus inevitably *reformist* and constitute no great threat to the *status quo.* This is evident, for example, even in an area where many Christians have shown considerable concern, namely the enforced mass removal of people. Many church people have condemned this practice as un-Christian on the grounds that it causes hardship, suffering, disruption of family life, etc. They then do not usually go further than appealing to the government to make adequate preparations for such removals and perhaps themselves providing some material aid for the victims. Some, though by no means all, of these people would be quite satisfied if the people were moved into typical township 'matchbox' houses. (They could hardly claim that *that* idea came from the Bible.)

All this is obviously a Christian thing to do. But, firstly, it is a politically-conditioned Christian response, and, secondly, it cannot be claimed to be *the* Christian response. There is no absolute Christian truth that says people should not be moved or that families should not be disrupted. The evacuation of women and children from cities during the war had these effects yet no one condemned it as un-Christian. In that case there was a reason for it, whereas in the case of 'resettlement' there is no valid reason. But the judgement as to whether or not there is a reason is a political and sociological one not a biblical or theological one; or rather it is all of these. Nationalists would, and do, argue that there is a valid reason for removing people and that it is in the interests of the people concerned. One cannot counter this argument by saying: 'But the Bible says you must not cause people suffering'. They would reply: 'We agree. But we are not *causing* suffering; some suffering is the unavoidable by-product of the achievement of a greater good'. Such argument could go on for ever without being resolved and the resettlement programme would continue - as indeed it does. It would not be resolved because the argument is not about the Bible; it is about politics.

The government's resettlement policy is part of the whole apartheid system. It has been devised as a means of more efficient control and more effective exploitation; it is not simply a sadistic aberration of Nationalists who have not read their Bible properly. Nationalists see such control as necessary for the safety of the White man and such exploitation as necessary for the economic security of the White man and this, for them, justifies any hardship or suffering involved. Such justification is made even easier if you assume, as some Nationalists appear to do, that family life is not so important to Blacks as it is to Whites; that Blacks have a greater capacity for enduring physical and emotional suffering than Whites have; and if you believe in various other myths about 'the Bantu'. (Such myths may have been originally due to ignorance or prejudice, but it is possible that they are now accepted as 'facts'. These myths have to be disposed of before people can even begin to hear what the Bible says.)

To oppose even one instance of a forced removal it is necessary to oppose the whole apartheid system, because removals, and the inevitable suffering involved, cannot be stopped or even made 'more humane' so long as the Grand Design of apartheid remains the goal. That is why they are wrong and why they would still be wrong even if, *per impossibile,* no suffering or disruption of families were involved. To appeal to the government's moral sense to stop them is futile, because they are essential to what the government considers 'moral'. While Christians must condemn the suffering and do their best to alleviate it, they cannot consider this to be a Christian action and any further action to be political.

The un-Christianness of the policy lies in its root cause not only in its obviously un-Christian effects; to condemn only the effects is to be party to the implementation of the actual policy. One cannot avoid the political implications of a truly Christian response by real or feigned ignorance of the political causes of the problem.

Being political is a dangerous occupation in South Africa and it is not only the Church that seeks refuge in political naivete. Following the riots in Soweto and elsewhere, many people suddenly became concerned about the lot of urban Africans. They were quick to point out, however, that this concern was personal and humanitarian, not political. A group of mining magnates and businessmen formed the Urban Foundation to provide educational and other facilities for urban Africans, but it was the facilities they were concerned with, not politics (cf. O. Kunene, *Sunday Tribune,* 12.12.76). But every facet of Africans' lives is determined by politics; the causes of the riots and of all Black oppression are political. To claim to keep politics out of a solution to these problems can only mean looking for a solution which does not unduly disrupt the *status quo.* The businessmen, in particular, could not have been so naive as to think that their actions were not political;

unless they believe that capitalism is a religion and not a political system.

The Church, therefore, in its condemnation of the Nationalists' government and in the little activity for change in which it does engage, is, whether it acknowledges it or not, incorporating a particular set of political and social values into its teaching and practice of Christianity. It is these values which are being challenged, not some abstract understanding of Christianity. For, as Schillebeeckx points out,

> In the light of cultural and social presuppositions, which are usually not critically reflected upon, but rather accepted unquestioningly, theologians and the church's teaching office can [therefore] draw a conclusion from the kerygma which is logically consistent, compelling and coherent according to the original presupposition, but which may not be valid if this social and cultural presupposition later appears to be wrong. The logically consistent conclusion then simply becomes superfluous. (*The Understanding of Faith*, pp. 18-19).

Church leaders might well believe, for example, that from all the Gospel says about the value of people and the importance of their relationships with one another, the only logical conclusion that can be drawn is that people should meet together as much as possible. They therefore encourage Blacks and Whites to meet together socially, for discussion, for worship, etc. Some even appear to believe that if every White befriended a Black all the problems òf South Africa would be solved. But, although the Gospel stresses the importance of personal relationships, it does not say how they are to be realised in a particular situation. That depends very much on the causes of the lack of proper relationships.

The sort of meeting between Blacks and Whites which the Church and other Christian organisations wish to foster, is not the simple application or consequence of Christian teaching; it necessarily presupposes that the main cause of the estrangement, to put it mildly, between Blacks and Whites is racial discrimination based on prejudice and ignorance. But this is a political presupposition. To reject this type of meeting, therefore, is not to reject Christian teaching, but to reject the political presupposition on which the consequent practice is based. If the main political problem is the conflict of interests between Blacks and Whites, as members of the exploited and exploiting classes respectively, such 'meeting' could be counter-productive both to the formation of genuine personal relationships and to solving the problems of South Africa; in that case it would not be a Christian form of action. What the main political problem is, is a political question and it cannot be assumed that the more reformist or liberal analysis is necessarily the Christian one.

There is a great danger that such 'meetings' will obscure the main issue for both Whites and Blacks. A Black man who needs the recognition of a White man to assure him of his humanity will never liberate himself. My befriending a Black man will not free him from the pass laws and the exploitation of his labour or give him the vote. It is these things that are dehumanising him, not the lack of a White 'friend'. As they are making more and more clear, Blacks do not want Whites to hold their hands, literally or figuratively, but to get off their backs.

This is not, of course, to say that one should encourage hostility between Blacks and Whites (such hostility is so entrenched and institutionalised in our society that it would be difficult for anyone to encourage it further), but rather that we should all be tackling the real political problems, each in his own way. When these are resolved personal relationships will hardly need to be an issue. If we are really doing this, personal relationships, the importance of which is not denied, will just happen; they will not have to be contrived.

Once we acknowledge that political, social and cultural presuppositions are an essential part of any Christian response, we must examine our present ones (though we will not be able to uncover them all) and make a definite and critical choice of the best methods of political analysis and means of action. We can only make this choice from those which are available to all men; we do not, as Christians, have our own. No such choice is unbiased and the Christian's cannot and should not be. The Christian's choice of political options should be biased by his concern for the poor and the oppressed, because God, in both the Old and the New Testaments, has shown Himself to be biased in favour of these, and they are the victims of injustice which is the denial of God. 'God always takes his stand unconditionally and passionately on this side and this side alone: against the lofty and in behalf of the lowly.' (Karl Barth).

If we are to take the same stand we obviously cannot assume a capitalist stance. Our first task therefore, as G. Arroyo explains that it was for Christians in Latin America, 'is a matter of identifying, in the dominant interpretation of the Christian message, the elements borrowed from bourgeois ideology; it is a matter of working to liberate the mass of Christians, who, through the penetration to their depths of a Christianity wedded to capitalist values, are blocked by the religion whose heirs they are from becoming aware of the causes of social problems and from adopting a liberating solution.' (*New Blackfriars*, Nov. 1974). (I have given only a few examples of the South African Church's unquestioning acceptance of liberal capitalist values. I leave it to someone more competent than I to do a more detailed study.) This does not mean that we reject the capitalist ideology and take over another political system *as an ideology*. As Arroyo concludes, 'it is a matter of showing, by our practice as much as by our words, that the Christian faith can and must become more and more at home in a socialist option, even if it cannot become enclosed within that option.' Christians must be critical of any ideology in the light of the biblical events and the values of the kingdom; but we can only give effect to these values in a specific historical context by making a definite political option.

The need for a definite political option, however, must not be made the excuse for an unending search for an ideal 'theory', which can only lead to intellectual discussion about 'the masses' and lose sight of the fact that the whole object of the exercise is how to love people. We are concerned with looking for the best available means of doing this. All such means are necessarily contingent; but that does not make them unimportant. They derive both their contingency and their importance from the fact that God became man in a *particular* time and place. Christians usually appear to conclude from this fact that we ought to live as if we were in that same time and place; whereas the obvious conclusion is that, since Christ incorporated the particularities of his time and place into his response to the Father, we should do the same in respect of *our* time and place.

It cannot, therefore, be stated categorically that one can only be a Christian by being a socialist, nor that one cannot be a Christian if one is a socialist; though either might be able to be said in a particular historical context, and the former, I shall argue, is true in ours. The only definitive thing one can say is that you can only be a Christian if you love your neighbour. But this is not religious or political 'theory'. Christians are not those who believe in loving one's neighbour, they are those who do. We are not told how we are to do this, but we are told why: because God first loved us. Christianity, therefore, consists basically in two facts: God's love for us and our love for our neighbour. And this is true whether one is a monk or a miner. There are not two distinct Christian responses; there is only one. This response, however, can be expressed in two different ways: by a 'monastic' approach or a 'secular' approach. The distinction is not between a 'religious' and a 'political' approach. Both the monastic and the secular approaches are religious and both are political.

An essential demand of the monastic approach is the rejection of the evils of society; and that is a political action. In former times it was possible to do this by literally and physically fleeing from society. It is at least questionable whether there is any place in the world today where one could escape from society. However, we are not concerned

here with those who actually become monks. But the monastic approach
has influenced the practice of Christians who continue to live in society.
Since these do not physically leave society, their rejection of its evils
must take another form. The Berrigans, for example, have shown how
this can be done by symbolic actions - such as by pouring blood on
draft cards. This is not a symbolic rejection, but a real rejection by
symbolic acts. Such actions obviously have political implications, even
though they are not based on a particular political analysis or judged in
terms of political strategy; they are seen simply as the expression of
one's religious convictions. One confronts the values held by society
and expressed by State actions with one's Christian values, regardless of
the political or other consequences. This is also the basis of the
Jehovah's Witnesses' stand in relation to the authority of the State.

Most White South African Christians, however, seek refuge from
their political obligations by appealing to a monastic-type spirituality,
but they do not follow the monastic practice of rejecting the evils of
society either physically or symbolically. In South African society even
a symbolic rejection would land people in jail - as the burning of Passes,
for example, did. If all White Christians who claim to believe in the
primacy of the spiritual were to draw the practical conclusion from
this they would all be in jail; and so be part of the solution by at least
not being part of the problem.

However, there is no reason for the practice of Christians who live in
society being determined by people who do not. A person who physically
lives in a society cannot avoid being part of that society; he shares in its
benefits and in its evils. He, therefore, has political responsibilities and
the discharging of these responsibilities is part of his being a Christian.
A secular approach, therefore, demands that one does not simply try to
dissociate oneself from the evils, which is impossible anyway, but that
one uses the most effective means available of overcoming them. Further,
the nature of modern society and of its evil practices is such that a
symbolic rejection is not sufficient. Firstly, a modern society can afford
to ignore and has the power to encapsulate symbolic actions. The
Nationalists, for example, could have afforded to ignore the Roman
Catholic Church's symbolic act of admitting a few Blacks to White
schools. They did not do so, but they are still able to 'encapsulate' it by
a slight adaptation of their policy and thus to render it ineffective.

There is no need for a political strategy to match the political
strategy of those defending the *status quo*, if one's rejection of the evils
of society is to be effective and real.

Secondly, the political and economic structures of modern society
are very complex; changing them is an equally complex matter. The
evils - war, poverty, racism, etc. - are obviously enough; but in order to

overcome them it is necessary to understand how they are caused and how they are perpetuated; this can only be done by means of a political analysis.

In order, therefore, to fulfil his religious obligation of loving his neighbour by overcoming the injustices that he suffers in society a Christian needs a political strategy and a political analysis. Whatever the case may be in other times and places, in South Africa at the present time the nature and extent of the evils of society are such that a Christian cannot effectively perform his Christian duty without adopting a political strategy and analysis.

He needs a strategy and analysis which can give historical form to his concern for the poor and oppressed in this particular situation. The choice of political strategy and analysis is determined by their effectiveness, which can only be judged by scientific norms, in giving practical expression to this concern. The evils of society are not simply caused by 'politics', but by a specific form of politics; if they are caused by capitalist politics, they can only be overcome by socialist politics, which then become an obligatory option for Christians.

Many Christians shy away from taking a definite and unashamedly biased political stance because they believe, perhaps sincerely, that this would be contrary to the demands of Christian reconciliation. But, as Bonino says, 'The ideological appropriation of the Christian doctrine of reconciliation by the liberal capitalist system in order to conceal the brutal fact of class and imperialist exploitation and conflict is one - if not *the* - major heresy of our time.' (*Doing Theology in a Revolutionary Situation,* p. 121). Christians look for the *final* reconciliation of men; in the meantime our task is to make it true that all men are one. We have to overcome the differences between men, not just ignore them.

Christ himself was, and is, 'a sign of contradiction' and he said that his followers would be rejected and persecuted. People are not rejected and persecuted if they spend all their time bending over backwards to avoid offending anyone, which is what Christian reconciliation often appears to be interpreted as meaning. Christ was not crucified for being 'nice' to people; he was a threat to both the religious and the secular authorities. Christian reconciliation is a task that has to be performed by removing the causes of conflict between men, not a doctrine to which we pay lip-service. The basic cause of conflict between men in the world today is that it is necessary for the majority to be poor so that the few might be rich. The Christian cannot decide that his role in this conflict is to be the referee. He, like everybody else, is part of the conflict and must therefore take sides. He should be unequivocally on the side of the poor and oppressed, so any attempt to avoid taking sides means in fact to side with the oppressors.

There are other lesser causes of conflict, but the Christian can never be a spectator of any conflict, no matter how much he might want to be; and this is not what is demanded of any agent of Christian reconciliation.

It is simply not possible to reconcile oppressor and oppressed; only people can be reconciled. Oppressor and oppressed alike can only become people in relation to each other when the oppressor-oppressed relationship has been destroyed. Destroying that relationship is part of the process of reconciliation, Christian or otherwise; reconciliation between oppressor and oppressed is a contradiction in terms. It is only the oppressed who can destroy this relationship and thus, as Freire says, liberate both themselves and the oppressor. The oppressor cannot be persuaded by other members of the oppressing class to stop being an oppressor, because, generally speaking, he does not believe that he is an oppressor and this belief cannot really be challenged so long as the oppressed themselves remain silent and acquiescent. Only if those whom he is oppressing reject his oppression will the oppressor be able to recognise the oppressive nature of his actions. Of course, if this rejection is successful, it will not matter very much whether he recognises this or not; he will no longer be an oppressor. Only then can reconciliation take place, because only then will they be able to see each other as people. Therefore, in supporting the oppressed in their rejection of oppression one is also helping the oppressor and is thus fulfilling one's Christian duty to both.

The resolution of the conflict of interests between the oppressors and the oppressed does not have to be violent, but there is always the possibility that it will be. This is certainly one aspect of any political option which a Christian will have to view critically; which he can do because he is not ideologically bound to any system. This is a difficult and, in South Africa particularly, a delicate question, which we cannot go into here.*

From what I have said about the historical nature of the Christian response, I think it should be obvious that I do not believe that anyone can give *the* Christian answer to the question, 'May a Christian use violence?' On such grounds, it is equally wrong to make either the use or non-use of violence an absolute ideal. Whether the use of violence in a particular situation can be the Christian response can only be decided in that situation. (Since this response is an attempt to realise the same truths and the same values realised by the normative responses of the biblical response, this is not a relativistic or purely subjective approach.)

---

* For a detailed study of the question, see J.G. Davies, *Christians, Politics and Violent Revolution*

There is no such thing as violence as such, so there is no point in trying to decide whether it is Christian or not as such. Non-violence is the ideal in the sense that it would obviously be better if peace and justice could be brought about without the use of violence, but it cannot be absolutised to rule out the use of any violence by any Christian in any circumstances.

In South Africa even the discussion of violence may be considered a criminal offence, carrying a minimum penalty of five years' imprisonment and a maximum of the death sentence. It is not perhaps surprising, therefore, that although our society is ridden with all forms of violence - legal, bureaucratic, personal, military - there are probably proportionately more professed pacifists in South Africa than anywhere else in the world. The Church's attitude towards violence is ambivalent, to say the least, and does not go beyond repeating that there are two traditions in Christian teaching, the majority view maintaining the just war theory and a minority upholding the pacifist tradition, and suggesting that Christians should consider whether they can in conscience participate in the present activities of the South African Defence Force. Many denominations, however, still second chaplains who hold rank in the Defence Force. And when prayers are said 'for the boys on the border' there is little doubt who 'the boys' are. (This is probably the only context where 'boys' does not refer to Africans.)

It tends to be assumed that government or institutionalised violence, particularly when executed by the armed forces, is easier to justify than violence of freedom fighters, though it might be condemned in particular instances. It seems to me, however, that it is easier to justify the activities of the freedom fighters as a Christian response to a particular situation than it is to justify institutionalised violence in the form of a standing army. It is the latter that idealises and indeed idolises violence. It is the perpetrators of institutionalised violence who bedeck their churches with regimental flags, who award medals to people for killing other people, who erect memorials and who continually relive old battles. Even if violence can sometimes be considered a Christian response, it can only be accepted as unfortunately the case and not gloried in as these practices imply. The distinction between 'idealising' and using violence is, I think, more important than that between institutionalised and revolutionary violence.

I find it difficult, emotionally, to accept that killing people can be an expression of love, but I also acknowledge the truth and cogency of Herbert McCabe's remarks:

There is an important and dangerous fallacy that Christians should always behave as though the Kingdom were already visibly established, and that if they do this the Kingdom will be brought about. Thus it is rather vaguely thought that if Christians, in spite of the evident fact that they are living in a particularly brutal and murderous phase of the decay of capitalism, resolutely pretend (or have 'faith') that they inhabit the Kingdom of God on earth, then capitalism will melt away and the true reality will be revealed. This fallacy underlies, for example, some forms of Christian pacifism. It is perfectly obvious that whatever we mean by the Kingdom it will not involve violence or any form of physical coercion, and that people will respond to each other in and because of love, but it does not follow from this that if we eschew all physical coercion now this will itself lead to a condition of greater justice and peace which will be a step towards the Kingdom. (*New Blackfriars*, Dec. 1974, p. 534).

I cannot say whether violence, in the form of rioting or guerrilla warfare, is a Christian response for the oppressed people of South Africa. I am not one of them and I cannot identify with their experience. I have been told many times by Blacks in the past that they would rather die than continue living in their oppressed condition; the Black youth have shown that this can be literally true. I might, in my better moments, be prepared to die, but life for me in this society is not so desperate that I would actually prefer to. If a person is suffering so much at the hands of others that he would prefer to die than endure it, how can anyone who is not suffering in that way dictate to him what he should do and gainsay his right to resort to violence? This is not to idealise violence, but to accept the possibility of its use as a regrettable necessity.

In the following chapters we will look at the political options available in South Africa. I am concerned with making a theological judgement on these options, not with the technicalities of putting a particular political system into effect. Political, economic, historical and other factors are an essential part of this judgement; but the practical technical details are the concern of other sciences and should be the subject of a separate study by experts in these fields. An initial study has been made by Dr Richard Turner in his book *The Eye of the Needle*, which is banned in South Africa, as is its author; but, if he could be quoted, I am sure that he would not claim that it is a definitive one.* Much of the groundwork for such a study was done some years ago by the 'Study Project on Christianity in an Apartheid Society' (SPROCAS). This project was partly sponsored by the churches, although its findings have never really been taken seriously by them.

SPROCAS' general approach was moderate and many of its

---

* Dr Richard Turner was shot dead in his home in January 1978.

recommendations could be seen as reformist; it aimed at consensus rather than a radical critique. It did, however, provide a great deal of data and raised a number of issues which could be the basis for on-going study, analysis and action. I am not saying that we must have a comprehensive analysis before we can do anything. Theory and practice are interdependent; our on-going analysis is deepened and crystallised in our actions and the direction and motivation of our action are clarified by our analysis. While SPROCAS was a step in the right direction, it had severe limitations. Firstly, although it was a highly academic analysis, it was concerned with the practical implications of problems and alternatives rather than with the underlying causes. It did to some extent tend to assume that racial prejudice was at the root of all the evils. Such an assumption has long been rejected by some and is being increasingly questioned. Some would see the race issue as irrelevant to what is exclusively a class struggle; more would see it as essentially a class struggle with race as an aggravating factor. We need, however, to take account of all the factors - economic, racial, cultural and religious - which generate dependency and further oppression. Secondly, SPROCAS, in common with virtually all academic analyses, was not based on any first-hand experience of or original research into the needs and aspirations of the worst victims of oppression. True, there were Black representatives on the various commissions, but they were there basically on White terms. The whole framework of the analysis was a White-conceived one and hence there tended to be an implicit acceptance of White values and no real account was taken of the values of the oppressed people themselves.

2·Politics and Theology

Introductory note

My primary concern in this section is to challenge the *assumption*, evident in the practice of most English-speaking Christians, that a 'liberal' interpretation of South African history and politics should determine a Christian's political involvement. In looking at the political options open to a Christian in South Africa we are not engaging in an academic, 'objective' analysis of historical facts. We are trying to find the most effective way of loving one's neighbour. We are, therefore, still engaged in a *theological* exercise. I am aware of the fact that there is considerable controversy in academic circles about some of the issues touched upon in the first two chapters and about the influence of other events which are not mentioned. However, a Christian, as a Christian, has no means of settling such a controversy, nor can he wait until there is a consensus among academics (which there probably never will be) before he decides what his Christian practice is going to be. A Christian's choice is not determined simply by the weight of academic argument behind a particular interpretation; nor, on the other hand, does it rest upon a blind acceptance of the view that happens to suit him.

I accept, on the one hand, that the 'radical' viewpoint taken here can be adequately supported by scientific arguments. I have not expounded them in detail because I am interested in making a practical theological judgement, not an academic one. (If the reader wishes to go into the arguments more deeply, I refer him to the full texts of the authors quoted and to the works listed in the extensive bibliography in H. Wright's *The Burden of the Present.*) On the other hand, I do not believe that *any* amount of academic argument can justify the 'liberal' interpretation. All such argument is invalidated if one rejects the normative value of capitalism on which this interpretation is based and which a Christian, I shall maintain, cannot accept. 'Liberal' interpreters claim complete objectivity for their viewpoint. But such objectivity is as impossible in history and political science as we have seen that it is in theology.

chapter 6
The Nationalist Option

The more radical opponents of the Nationalist regime, particularly
overseas critics, are often accused, not only by the Nationalists
themselves but also by moderate opposition groups, of applying double
standards in their criticisms of South Africa. Black and/or Communist
States can repress and even massacre people, yet the critics remain silent,
whereas South Africa's every crime, however small, is vociferously
condemned. Some try to turn this into a left-handed compliment by
saying that this is because higher standards are expected of South Africa
since it is a 'Christian' and 'civilised' country. These claims mean nothing
to me and I am sure they do not to other critics.

It is true that there is oppression and exploitation in other countries,
in fact, in virtually every other country. The difference, however, lies
not so much in the nature of what the Nationalists do as in its extent
and its rationalisation. The whole of the Black population is oppressed
and this is done in order to retain political and economic power in the
hands of a minority whose only 'claim' to such power is the colour of
their skin. It is the end which the Nationalists have in view rather than
the means they use to achieve it that makes South Africa unique. The
means which the Nationalists have used and still use are much the same
as the means used by every would-be imperialist power - conquest,
domination and exploitation; not that this makes them any less
reprehensible. And in South Africa they have been applied more
extensively and more intensively, because of an irrational desire to
exclude the vast majority of the population from *any* share in the power.

There is, therefore, in the Nationalist system an irrational element
and a very large racist element. This, however, does not mean that we
are dealing simply with a bunch of insane and/or immoral racists. South
Africa has been built up into a modern, industrialised society, with a
complex (and very efficiently oppressive) political system and with

considerable military power. All this is not the product of racism, insane or otherwise. Capital, skill, technology, etc., have all played their part. But none of these could have achieved anything without, not only labour, but grossly exploited labour. The important thing about this labour was not, and is not, the colour of the people concerned, but their exploitability. The Blacks who are 'allowed' to stay in 'White' areas are just as Black as Mr Froneman's* 'surplus appendages' or the Department of Bantu Administration's 'non-productive Bantu', who are dumped in the 'homelands'.

Politics are about power; Nationalist politics are about White power. The desire for White power and the exclusion of Blacks from power is obviously racist. But one cannot explain this desire for power, or the steps taken to gain it, by saying that it was because the first settlers were racists. They did not want White power because they were racists; they were racists because they wanted White power.

The need of one group to claim superiority over another group can only arise when its status or interests are actually or potentially challenged or threatened. (There would be no point in even Muhammed Ali claiming to be the greatest if nobody else had any interest in boxing.) The status or interests of one race group are not threatened by the *race* of another group. Race is not in itself a cause of conflict; though today this is not immediately obvious, because the effect of propaganda, racial myths and the actual practice of racial discrimination has been to identify many other unconnected 'threats' with the race of the people who pose them. If two groups come into conflict there must be something over which they conflict; there must be something in which both have an interest in having for themselves.

The first interest of the White settlers was land. This, inevitably, conflicted with the interest of those who already had the land. Even if these settlers had believed that they had a right, divinely or otherwise given, to the land, the form which the conflict took would still have been determined by historical circumstances; among which was the fact that those who wanted the land were White and those who already had it were Black. Nor would such a belief explain the outcome of the conflict; for people cannot physically dominate other people just because they believe they have the right to do so.

White domination was not achieved, nor can it be maintained, simply by discriminating against Blacks. It is not possible to discriminate against people unless you have power over them; otherwise why should those discriminated against put up with it? This power was first imposed militarily. The history of South Africa is a history of wars over land.

---

* The then (1969) Deputy Minister of Justice, Mines and Planning.

The first White settlers and their descendants were not interested in the biological, genetic, cultural, or any other features of the people who had the land. They took the land because they wanted it as a source of wealth, not because they thought that the Africans were incapable of looking after it or were undeserving of it because they were inferior. They were able to take the land because they had superior weapons. But these 'wars were a process which gave the white community more than possession of the bulk of the best land. It gave them a considerable measure of control over the services of the natives. The land wars were also labour wars. In other words, the natives lost free access to the land, but were permitted to draw sustenance from it as labourers, herdsmen, tenants and renters.' (De Kiewiet, *A History of South Africa: Social and Economic,* p. 180; quoted in Johnstone, *Class, Race and Gold,* p. 21). This 'control over the services of the natives' was gradually extended and entrenched by political means. The ideological formulation of these means came later and was intended to 'rationalise' the position and to provide a 'moral justification' for the practice of exploitation.

If we leave aside the ideological embellishments, we can see that what the early settlers, the Voortrekkers, and present-day Nationalists share is the same basic objective: the control of political power as the means of protecting their economic interests. The achieving of this objective, however, has been, and is being, determined by much more mundane considerations than divine mandates.

When the present Nationalist government came to power in 1948 the nature of society had changed completely since the time of the Voortrekkers and Afrikanerdom had changed with it. In the interim the conquerors had themselves become the conquered and this, together with other more natural factors, had forced a great number of Afrikaners to become workers. British domination of economic, and to a certain extent, political power had made many of these the 'less privileged' section of the working class. On the other hand, others had developed alternative capitalist means to the ownership of land for making money; others again had held on to the land. The Nationalists therefore had a diversity, though not a conflict, of interests to protect against the common threat of the *'Swart Gevaar'.* They had, however, already learnt about accommodating ideology to the demands of their economic interests.

The basic structures of South Africa's racially discriminatory society were set up long before the present Nationalists came into power. When land was the only source of wealth the threat from Blacks could be contained by physical force and later by the comparatively simple means of 'anti-vagrancy' laws. These controlled the movement of Blacks and made it impossible for them to survive without working for Whites.

The development of mining and industrial capitalism, however, 'necessitated' the creation of much more complex controls in order to mobilise Black labour while at the same time protecting the interests of both the White capitalists and the White workers. Blacks were excluded from any share in political power; they were denied any bargaining power by the provisions of the Industrial Conciliation Act. Job reservation was 'legalised' and, under the so-called 'civilised labour' policy, Whites were given preference, and higher wages, even for unskilled work in government services, notably the railways. The movement of Blacks was further controlled by increasingly stringent 'Pass Laws'. The recommendations of the 1922 Stallard Commission, which were based on the principle that Africans could only enter White areas for the purpose of serving the Whites, would be acceptable to the most *'verkrampte'* present-day Nationalist. And, of course, the basic cause of all friction and hostility in South Africa - ownership of the land - was given 'legal' form in the Land Acts of 1913 and 1936, which reserved 87 per cent of the land for White ownership.

All these, and many other similar, measures might be described as simply racist. No doubt racial prejudice was, and still is, responsible for the harshness and callousness of some of the measures and the way they have been implemented, but it cannot explain why they were introduced. That can only be explained by the fact that the White capitalists and White workers soon found that they had a common interest in exploiting Black workers. It was in the interests of the employers to divide the workers so that they would not unite against them and make demands for all workers. This division took place on racial lines because the Blacks were already discriminated against: they had no political power and had been made completely dependent economically on the Whites. The first White workers, who were predominantly English-speaking immigrants, could demand higher wages because they were skilled both in their work and in trade unionism. At that stage they were in conflict with both the capitalist employers and with all unskilled workers, Black or White. However, to safeguard this position they also needed effective political power and this could only be attained by joining forces with the Afrikaans-speaking workers, who, while being unskilled and hence a threat, did have the vote and were even more threatened by the vast, cheap, Black labour force.

The quest for political power was led by the English-speaking skilled workers, but what is important to note is that 'The Afrikaans workers responded socially and politically in terms of their perceived economic interests, displaying a healthy interest in working class organisations, and appear to have voted solidly for the Labour Party. They made *no attempt* to organise themselves along cultural, "Christian-National" lines.' (D. O'Meara, *South Africa Labour Bulletin,* April 1975). Their quest was at least partially successful when, after the 1924 General Election, the Labour Party had enough seats to form a coalition with the National Party in the Pact government, which was responsible for most of the discriminatory measures against Blacks already referred to.

The Pact government represented the interests of Afrikaner farmers and nascent capitalists and of the White workers in general over against the increasing power of the mining capitalists. It served the latter group by making the further exploitation of Blacks possible and the former groups by assisting in the formation of a national bourgeoisie. When the coalition broke up in 1933, it was the national bourgeois element of the National Party which formed the 'purified' National Party, while the rest joined with Smuts' South African Party in the formation of the United Party, which became increasingly the political arm of the mining capitalists. Although the Labour Party drew its support from all White workers, its official representatives were drawn almost exclusively from the skilled English-speaking workers. To preserve the political power they had attained in the Pact government, these aligned themselves with the United Party and thus with the mining capitalists. This common interest secured further their privileged position. At the same time, however, it led them to compromise the interests of the unskilled, predominantly Afrikaans-speaking workers.

After 1933, the Afrikaner workers and *petite bourgeoisie* were thus the only two groups of Whites who were not benefiting to their satisfaction from the exploitation of Blacks. The only way the *petite bourgeoisie* of the 'purified' National Party could gain their 'share' was to mobilise these workers - about whom they had not been previously concerned - firstly, to raise capital to enable them at least to begin to compete with the English-speaking capitalists and to provide employment opportunities for middle-class Afrikaners; secondly, to gain political power. However, there was, as O'Meara points out,

> one serious flaw in this scheme. Despite sustained attempts at cultural mobilisation, Afrikaans-speaking workers displayed a dangerous tendency to act in terms of class rather than cultural interests. To respond as workers - admittedly protected from and therefore hostile to the aspirations of Black workers, but as workers none the less - rather than as Afrikaners. The basis of this tendency was the trade union organisations, led by English-speaking artisans and dominated by the craft unions, which clearly had no interest in cultural mobilisation. Afrikaans workers thus belonged to class organisations, had their interests articulated in these terms and voted for the Labour Party. They thus had to be weaned from both. (*loc.cit.,* p. 44).

Thanks largely to the machinations of Albert Hertzog, they finally were; and it was the votes of former Labour Party supporters in six mining constituencies that secured the 1948 General Election for the Nationalists. Hertzog was assisted in his task by the increasing discontent of the Afrikaans-speaking workers with the Labour Party, which was seen to be more interested in its alliance with the mining capitalists than in the protection of their interests. The other decisive factor was the increasing 'threat' of the Black work force, which had grown not only in numbers but also in skills and political awareness. The Nationalists undertook to protect White workers by further entrenching racial discrimination as the means of averting this 'threat'.

The Nationalists did not have to invent racial discrimination; nor, on the other hand, were they tied, either in the efforts to gain power or in their exercise of it, to any immutable religious, cultural or political ideology, which they were in honour bound to implement to preserve the heritage handed down to them by their forebears. Any White group that has held political power in South Africa has had only one mandate: to protect White interests against Blacks. The Afrikaner Nationalists were, and are, no exception. 'It is obvious, but equally needs constant reiteration, that Afrikaner nationalist ideology developed historically as a *response to social change,* and is no immutable *Weltanschauung.*' (O'Meara, *op.cit.,* p. 48).

A detailed study of South Africa's political history would be necessary to confirm O'Meara's comment. I have only touched upon some aspects of this history in very sketchy fashion. But even this is sufficient I think to give substance to the warning that any current or future adaptation of the ideology of apartheid should not be interpreted as it is by many people both within and outside South Africa, as 'progress'. The Nationalists have always been prepared to adapt - provided their own interests have warranted it. This is perhaps the main difference between the National Party and the Herstigte National Party. The latter is hidebound by an earlier formulation of Nationalist ideology; whereas the former is realistic enough to appreciate that that formulation can no longer protect the same interests.

Complete control of political power is far more important to the Nationalists than it is to English-speaking capitalists, or to the few Afrikaner capitalists who no longer need government support in order to compete with their English-speaking counterparts. This is because the economic interests of the Nationalists: constituency - workers, farmers and employees of the vast State bureaucracies (which appear to employ almost everybody who votes Nationalist) - are entirely dependent on Nationalist control of political power. What would happen to the Afrikaner working class if a 'pure' capitalist government assumed power and proceeded to denationalise the railways and to hand over Iscor and other State-owned corporations to private enterprise? What would happen to both the workers and the farmers if there was a Black government, which would not only remove any form of job reservation but would also redistribute the land? For the Nationalists more than for any other group, both for historical reasons and because of the class interest of their constituents, *political power and economic interests are inextricably intertwined.* They will never, therefore, voluntarily relinquish, or even share, political power.

When the Nationalists gained power they were under an obligation to their supporters effectively to counter the 'threat' of growing Black militancy. Building on the existing racialist structures - which they, of course, had had a considerable hand in forming - was, to them, the obvious, and indeed only, way of doing this. However, the more ruthlessly they acted to show they could fulfil their promise to control the 'Black menace', the more they generated other threats: increased Black hostility and growing criticism and pressure from a small but vociferous minority of Whites within South Africa and from overseas countries. They therefore found it necessary both to adapt their policies and to provide a 'moral' justification for their basic objective. In respect of the latter, the Dutch Reformed Churches have played much the same sort of role as other churches did in Europe and the Americas for capitalism and slavery. (Is there really very much difference between a Roman Catholic Cardinal blessing a nuclear submarine and the Dutch Reformed Churches blessing apartheid?)

The Nationalists can afford to adapt their policies, provided this does not weaken their grip on political power. They have no vested interest in racial discrimination as such; and 'ethnic purity' without wealth and power would have no appeal to anybody. Thus, as their hold on power became firmer, they were able to make apartheid less crude and so allay some criticisms of their policies. But from 1950 to 1977 the pattern has been the same: any 'concessions' given to Blacks have been more than counter-balanced by increased political oppression. The Suppression of Communism Act, the banning of the ANC and PAC, the Terrorism Act, the Internal Security Act and numerous other repressive measures have left Blacks today with even less political freedom than they had in 1948. This is not compensated for by a slight increase in earnings and the removal of a few 'Whites only' signs. This history of South Africa has shown that economic advance does not necessarily bring political freedom. The Nationalists, therefore, are not directly threatened by the economic prosperity of some Blacks; in fact they can use this to show the 'justness' of their policies. Their power, both economic and political, is threatened by the political aspirations of Blacks.

The role of some opposition groups, particularly the English Press, seems to be confined to chiding the government for its slowness in removing 'petty' apartheid and to pointing out the illogicality of removing it in one area and not in another. They hail it as a victory when a Black is not actually physically thrown out of an hotel; and the inclusion of a Black in a Provincial cricket team heralds the end of apartheid. The Nationalists should, and perhaps they do, welcome such 'opposition', because it is helping them to make their system work more smoothly, without in any way threatening their power. They receive the same assistance from the people who seek to gain 'concessions' by making representations to the government. Thus, for example, the action of the leaders of the Anglican Church in seeking to come to some arrangement with the government about admitting children of all races to their schools even if it should succeed would be counter-productive. They are not asking the government to change any fundamental principle of its policy. To accord a 'privileged' status to the few Blacks who could afford to go to private Church schools would simply make the general policy work better. And 'when a system is irrational, sheer increase in efficiency tends to make its conditions worse, much worse - on occasion calamitous.' (Alves, *Tomorrow's Child,* p. 63). The only Blacks who would benefit would be the very few who would possibly receive a better education. But the government would be better able to 'rationalise' the position of the vast majority. No one can be given permission to violate government policy. If the government should agree, it would no longer be against their policy; the policy would have been adopted. But the Nationalists, as experience has shown, only do this when it is to their advantage.

The 'concessions' which the Nationalists can make are obviously limited by the interests of the people who keep them in power. There is no *ideological* reason, for example, why the National Party leadership should not form an alliance with English-speaking capitalists, as some of their predecessors did, but this would not be in the interests of the large working-class section of their *present* constituency and so they would lose support. They are further limited by the self-perceived interests of their supporters, who might interpret *any* move away from racial discrimination as a threat to their protected position.

On the other hand the ruthless measures applied to retain power by the suppression of all Black political opposition have to be explained to the rest of the world and, perhaps, to their own consciences. It is not surprising, therefore, that Nationalist propaganda is often confusing and contradictory. They are trying to assure one group that they are not moving away from racial discrimination and another group that they are. For the latter purpose we have 'progressed' from *baaskap,* through apartheid and separate development to plural democracy, all of which are smokescreens laid down to hide their basic objective and to 'justify' the means employed to attain it. So much effort has been put into this exercise and it is so important for their retention of power that their 'explanations' be accepted, that many Nationalists have no doubt come to believe them themselves. Only this can explain some of the government's more irrational actions. Some of the Nationalists' contradictory statements and stances, however, are not as irrational as they may at first appear. Although they are not presently prepared to enter into any form of political alliance with the 'enlightened capitalists', the latter do wield considerable influence because of their economic power. The government, therefore, cannot afford to alienate them completely.

The Nationalists' ability both to 'adapt' and to believe their own propaganda is illustrated by their policy in regard to 'independent homelands' - the biggest and probably most effective smokescreen of all. Nationalists now speak, with apparent sincerity, as if the setting up of 'independent homelands' were the logical conclusion of their policy, the fulfilment of an ideological dream, and the only just solution to the problems and conflicts of South Africa. But, according to the architect of the whole scheme, Dr Verwoerd, this was a *departure* from policy: 'The Bantu will be able to develop into separate states. This is not what we would have liked to see. It is a form of fragmentation that we would not have liked if we were able to avoid it.' It was considered necessary, however, in order to buy 'for the White man his freedom and the right to retain domination in what is his country' (*Hansard*, 4 April 1961).

It was for some time in the interests of the White economy that the Reserves remained undeveloped in order to 'entice' Africans into the labour market. The Reserves were not simply neglected out of a callous indifference to the welfare of Africans; it was a deliberate, and even more callous, policy. It is now in the interests of the same White economy, and of Nationalist politics, that Blacks be forcibly removed from 'White' areas. Any current development of the Reserves or 'homelands' fulfils a two-fold purpose: it keeps some Blacks happy and so helps to defuse the political threat, and it serves the interest of the White economy.

The pragmatic nature of the Nationalists' policy was further illustrated by Vorster's detente exercise. Despite the failure of that exercise, the Nationalists still have some room to manoeuvre before finally being driven into a corner, or perhaps into a *laager*. They still have a long way to go to fulfil their ambassador's promise made to the United Nations in 1974: 'My government does not condone discrimination purely on grounds of race or colour and we shall do everything in our power to move away from discrimination based on colour.' They will doubtless do sufficient at least to give the appearance of trying to fulfil this promise; and the West will be very patient, because 'You can't expect everything to change overnight.' There is also the obvious rationalisation that they are not concerned with 'race' or 'colour' but with 'nations', and they are not 'discriminating' against them but 'recognising' their 'right to sovereignty'. However, the Nationalists have not retracted, and I am sure they will not retract, the threat made by Strijdom,* likewise at the United Nations in 1950, that Whites 'will fight to the last drop of our blood to maintain White supremacy in South Africa'.

The Nationalists are quite capable of coping with the 'moralising' of the West and of White opposition groups, including the churches. The only real threat to the Nationalists, apart from the possibility of a full-scale invasion, stems from the heightened political awareness and resentment of Blacks, which has led to a complete rejection of the present system and can only express itself in an escalation of internal unrest. This threat cannot be countered by improving the material conditions of Blacks, whether this is done by the government or by well-meaning White liberals. It is the cause of the conditions, not simply the conditions themselves, which is the problem. This can only be solved by Blacks having the power to improve their own conditions. And this is on a national level, not by means of domesticated 'self-help schemes'.

This threat clashes head-on with the Nationalists' basic objective and I believe that we have not yet begun to see the lengths to which they will be prepared to go in order to overcome it. On their terms, the Nationalists can only react by ruthlessly crushing all political opposition. By political opposition I mean *anything* which fosters or is an expression of Black awareness of the true nature of their oppression; not 'opposition' which seeks only to gain 'concessions'. Meanwhile, other Blacks will be free to patronise five-star hotels and theatres and to build themselves palaces in the 'homelands'. The Nationalists can only hope that the number of these will increase.

However, in order to placate overseas and local critics, the suppression of political opposition will have to be carried out more stealthily than it has been in the past. Steps in this direction have already been taken by the Internal Security Act, which provides for the names of those detained being withheld. The far-reaching powers of censorship contained in the Defence Amendment Bill, which at the time of writing is before parliament but the passing of which is a mere formality, will ensure complete secrecy about any repressive measures which are taken.

*   Prime Minister of South Africa at the time.

And there can be no doubt that there will be many such measures.

From a political point of view, the Nationalists have everything to lose and nothing to gain by changing. They will cling desperately to power, not simply because of a fanatical belief in their racial 'purity', but because everything which they have acquired, by fair means or, mainly, foul, depends on it. The Nationalist government will not disintegrate because of its own moral turpitude; nor will it change in response to the moral exhortations of the Churches and others. I can see no grounds for the facile optimism of many, which is based on no more than the assumption that change *will* come because it *must* come. As Christians we believe that good will ultimately triumph over evil, but we have no assurance about when it will; nor do we have any divinely revealed guide as to how it will do so in this particular situation. White opposition groups appear to pay very little attention to this last question - the actual logistics of change. The Nationalists are clearly determined to hold on to power *at all costs.* This determination is backed up by the control of powerful military and paramilitary forces and a vast police and bureaucratic oppressive machinery. No amount of pleading or moral pressure can weaken that determination; only confrontation with an equally strong determination can do it.

Lacking such a determination, many people are turning to 'the economy' as the great force for change. Since most people, myself included, do not really understand how a national economy works, there is a tendency to attribute quasi-magical powers for good or ill to its development or collapse, depending on one's point of view. The economy, we are told by opposition politicians, cannot continue to bear the costs of the government's policies; therefore, the Nationalists must change. All we have to do is convince the Nationalists that this is the case and they will change. The Nationalists, however, can see that such a course of action would be of more benefit to the proponents of this argument, who represent English-speaking capitalists: interests, than it would to themselves. If the Nationalists were to change they would certainly lose everything; if they keep on fighting to retain power they can at least console themselves with the hope of winning.

The state of the economy will, however, obviously play a large part in the process of change. I am assured by economists that there are in fact no signs of an imminent collapse of the economy; though it is not as healthy as it was once assumed to be. In any event, other countries seem to survive with economies in various stages of collapse. The Rhodesian economy has been ailing for some time and the Ugandan economy surely gave up the ghost long ago, but this alone did not bring Smith to his knees and Amin is not noticeably troubled by it. The decline of the economy will only be of real concern to the Nationalists when they are forced to cut down on the costs of implementing their repressive measures and on the Defence budget. In terms of their priorities, however, there are numerous other areas where cuts can, and doubtless will, be made before these are affected. Perhaps the fact that they might well be the first to be affected explains the capitalists' concern for the economy.

Nationalist supporters and sympathisers are being conditioned, by the steady building-up of a war psychosis, to accept the necessity of 'making sacrifices for their country'. The response of many 'good' Catholics to their Bishops' support of the right to conscientious objection showed the degree of sympathy and support that the Nationalists have succeeded in arousing by their continual propaganda about the communist bogey and 'barbarous terrorists'. All good White South Africans would respond, financially and otherwise, to an appeal to meet this threat. Even on the economic front, therefore, the Nationalists still have some leeway.

Whites, however, will not be able, or expected, to meet all the costs. But the shifting of some of the cost of their own repression on to the Blacks could only result in increased Black opposition and 'unrest'. This would 'necessitate' further repression, which would cause further economic decline leading to even more 'unrest' and so it would continue until either there was nobody left to create unrest or no money for further repression. For how long this could continue nobody knows, but I do not believe that there is any likelihood of the Nationalists ever admitting defeat.

This is indeed a fearful, but I believe realistic, prospect. And there is absolutely no chance of preventing it unless people, both in South Africa and overseas, start to tackle the real problem of our society: the exploitation of the people and of the natural resources of South Africa by and for the Whites. Foreign investors and trading partners, Black and White capitalists and all who share in the fruits of the exploitation of the vast majority of the population are all part of the problem. The Afrikaner Nationalists are not noticeably more racist or more money-grabbing than anyone else, but, because of the nature of their money-grabbing, they are prepared to go to far greater lengths to keep power in their own hands than are those who do not need political control in order to protect their economic interests. They are, therefore, the major part of the problem and are more easily identifiable as such.

There is no need to demonstrate the un-Christian character of the Nationalist system. Whether racial discrimination is an end in itself or simply a means, it is still immoral and is condemned as such by all but a very small minority of Christians. But the end which the Nationalists are pursuing would be just as evil whatever the means used to achieve it.

To condemn only the means is to encourage·them to find more acceptable means of furthering the same immoral purpose. If the condemnation is to be effective and if the rejection of the system is to be real, as they have to be if they are to constitute a Christian response, it is necessary to attack the root cause of the evil. Most Christians are not doing this at present because of their unquestioning acceptance of the capitalist model of society, which, as we shall see in the next chapter, is both ineffective as a means of bringing about the radical change needed in South Africa and an unacceptable alternative for a Christian.

It is my contention, though by no means mine alone, that Christians, as well as others, can only, firstly, expose and, secondly, begin to face up to, the cause of the evils of our society by adopting a socialist political perspective. It is not possible to be opposed to what is clearly an evil system on purely moral, non-political grounds. Such 'opposition' cannot but become lost in the smokescreen of Nationalist propaganda. More importantly, any attempt to exclude political action also excludes the historical verification which is demanded by the nature of a Christian response. Our belief in the Christian doctrine of the dignity and equality of all men can only be made true for us by our using the most effective means available to ensure that this dignity and equality are *in fact* recognised. It is not sufficient, therefore, simply to condemn the Nationalists. We must reject their whole system and seek to give practical effect to our beliefs within another political framework.

chapter 7
The Enlightened Capitalist Option

At present virtually all White opposition, including that of the Churches, to the Nationalist regime is working towards the enlightened capitalist 'solution'. Such opposition seeks to do away with racial discrimination and to eliminate the more obvious injustices of the present system. The efforts of the enlightened capitalists consist of protesting against these injustices and trying to persuade the Nationalists to see the moral evil and the economic disadvantages of their ways. Their primary concern is to maintain their economic and social status with an easy conscience. If they could persuade the Nationalists to adapt their policy sufficiently to eliminate the blatant injustices to which it gives rise, they would be satisfied. They can see, however, that this is becoming an increasingly remote possibility and that the best means of protecting their interests is to win Black support for their version of capitalism.

The degree of change which would satisfy the enlightened capitalists would also be sufficient to gain the approval of American and Europe, since they too are primarily concerned with preserving their own investments in, and trade and other relations with, South Africa without being open to the obviously justified criticism of their more socially aware citizens. The managing director of Nedbank was no doubt right when he said: 'We have many good friends overseas and really few enemies. Our friends are all very sympathetic, but wherever I travel they ask us to make it easier in our policies and actions for them to be our friends. The concessions required are not revolutionary . . . It is so often rather petty actions we take in individual instances that embarrass our friends so much.' (*Rand Daily Mail,* 13 Oct. 1976, Mr G. Muller). These 'friends' are easily placated because they want to be placated. While there are some exceptional individuals, even among politicians and perhaps even among businessmen, Western governments and business as a whole are not concerned about the welfare of the Blacks in South Africa. They are concerned with their own interests and it is in their interests that South Africa has a respectable image.

Big business, on which this opposition is currently pinning much of its faith, obviously needs to support such change. The more honest businessmen admit that their efforts to improve African wages and working conditions, to provide educational and other facilities, etc., are in their own interests and are an investment for their own future. Mr Oppenheimer argued this case very suavely and plausibly in his 1975 Chairman's address and at an Investment Conference organised by the *Financial Mail.* He argued that directors of businesses had the right to use some of the shareholders' profits for improving the 'environment' in which they operated and said: 'The circumstances of South Africa are such that I would judge that a comparatively high level of environmental investment - which is a more accurate term than "charitable donations" to describe what I have in mind - would be required than in most other industrialised countries.' (*Financial Mail,* Special Survey, 6 June 1975). Mr David Lurie stated the position more bluntly and, I think, more accurately:

> A business has one primary duty - that is to survive. It has to survive (and after that preferably to grow) in the society in which it exists. To do this it has to function, perform and contribute to its environment in a manner best calculated to ensure *its self-interest.* . . To survive it has to do the following:
> □ Pay its workers a sufficiently competitive wage rate;
> □ Train its labour *so that the business may be more prosperous,* or at least more competitive;
> □ Try to affect the environment so that the labour force is stable; and
> □ Try to generate, amongst its employees by any means in its power, a larger class of 'haves' rather than 'have-nots', so that these, in their self-interest, will want to perpetuate the *status quo* rather than to destroy it. . .
> South Africa, particularly in the modern world, needs for survival an increasing *non-White* middle class. Only with a sound middle class can any society prosper and grow and be essentially conservative. There are *simply not enough Whites* in South Africa to make up the middle; *we* need the Coloureds, Indians and Blacks to perpetuate *our* frankly conservative and capitalist society. (*Financial Mail,* p. 40; my italics).

Mr Lurie at least implies that if there were enough Whites there would be no need to bother about the Blacks; Blacks are there to be *used* to bolster up the upper class of Whites. But at least we have here an honest statement of the aims of South African capitalism.

The Chamber of Mines was not quite so explicit as Mr Lurie, but its intention was equally clear, when it announced that it intended pressing for family housing and various other 'perks' for the *top 10 per cent* of employees on the mines. This was hailed by many as 'progress'. But it is clearly more in the interests of the mining houses to share a very small part of their wealth with 10 per cent than ultimately to have to share all its wealth with 100 per cent.

It is not only businessmen who are, in effect, asking Blacks to come to their rescue; opposition politicians are doing it too. The businessmen offer the Blacks some 'reward' for their co-operation; the politicians have nothing to offer. It is a favourite theme of both United Party and Progressive-Reform Party politicians that Whites and Blacks must stand together to combat the threat from outside the country. (See, for example, Colin Eglin, *Sunday Tribune,* 9 Jan. 1977.) This seems to me to be a strangely unpersuasive argument. I do not know of any Blacks who see any *threat* from outside; they see *liberation* coming from outside. Many of those outside are the sons/daughters, mothers/fathers, brothers/sisters, or wives/husbands of Black South Africans, so why should they feel threatened? The threat is to Whites. White politicians, therefore, are simply asking Blacks to protect them.

The enlightened capitalists, of course, see nothing wrong in protecting their own self-interest. They would claim that in so doing, in making profits, they are also acting in the interest of the whole community by providing employment, 'improving the environment', and, if the Chairman of Bradlows is to be believed, simply by making profits: 'it should be constantly emphasised that businessmen benefit the community most by establishing successful enterprises which earn large profits' (*Financial Mail,* 6 June 1975). The profits that they have made so far have not only not benefited the community as a whole, but they have been made at the expense of the vast majority of the members of that community. The system of racial discrimination which had been built up to protect the interests of the White landowners was used and extended to further the interests particularly of the mining industry, from which the wealth of the present enlightened capitalists largely derives.

The discovery of diamonds and gold and the consequent growth of industrialisation and the development of cities created the need for skilled labour, which was mainly drawn from overseas, and for a vast amount of unskilled labour. By this time there were a number of Whites who did not have land and others who thought that they would make money more quickly on the mines. These were no more skilled than the African workers drawn from the 'Reserves' and so were in direct cheap labour. It was admitted by the mining industry at the time and has never been denied that the mines would never have been an economic proposition without ultra-cheap labour. How did it happen that Blacks supplied the cheap labour while Whites made a lot of money? Why were White workers, who were themselves technically being exploited, able to acquire a share in the fruits of the gross exploitation of Blacks? We have already touched on this question in the previous chapter; to answer it fully would require a detailed study of the history of the relationships between Black and White workers and an analysis of the relative roles played in the whole social system by political and economic factors. (A brief account is given in Turner, *Eye of the Needle,* pp. 22-31. An intensive academic study relating specifically to the gold mines is to be found in Johnstone's *Class, Race and Gold.*) It is clear, however, that the capitalist mineowners did not simply go about their business and the politicians about theirs. It was not a case of the capitalists being concerned with the economic growth and the politicians with racial discrimination. There would have been no economic growth without racial discrimination and racial discrimination would not have been intensified in the way it was if it had not been for the needs of economic growth.

By this time there were far more Africans in the 'Reserves' than were 'needed' by the White landowners. Mr Oppenheimer gives the impression that the mining industry did these people a favour by providing employment for them. He tells less than half the story when he says, 'The mass of the workers . . . consisted of Black peasants, unskilled and totally inexperienced in industrial life, attracted by wages which, while miserably low, were nevertheless more than they could earn in the depressed rural areas from which they came.' (*Financial Mail,* 6 June 1975). Left to themselves they would not have needed to earn any more. But they were not left to themselves either by the government or by the mining industry, who between them exerted considerable 'push' - which was a far more significant factor than any attraction which the mines' 'miserably low' wages held.

The government had already introduced taxation, which removed the last vestiges of economic independence from Africans and made it necessary for them to work for Whites for a cash wage. There were also other push factors such as population growth and the shortage of land. The land shortage was not simply the consequence of population growth. The African population had been left with little enough land after the Whites had taken their 'share', and their rights were further curtailed by the 1913 Land Act which debarred them from ever being able to acquire title to property in 'White' South Africa.

But the existing labour mobilisation mechanisms, together with these 'push' factors were not sufficient in themselves to produce the quantity of African workers sought by the mining companies. The companies therefore developed their own system of mobilising Africans into mine labour - a system of loan advancement and debt inducement. According to the President of the Chamber of Mines, it was only through 'paying out large sums to recruiters, who in turn endeavour to induce the natives to come to work by offers of loans and the wherewithal to pay their taxes and their debts to the local traders who have given them credit, that we have been able to keep up the supply of labour to what it is today'. (Johnstone, *op.cit.,* pp. 27-8).

The mines needed not only cheap labour, but *very* cheap labour. This could only be obtained from Blacks; not only because the Whites had some political power and were thus in a stronger bargaining position, but also because of their respective economic positions. 'It was impossible, given that Whites did not receive a subsidy from the land in the way that black migrants did, to push the white wages down to the required ultra cheap level of the black workers.' (K. Kolbe, *South Africa Labour Bulletin,* vol.3, No.3, p. 85). Then, as now, the poorest section of the community, the 'Reserves', subsidised the richest, the mining houses. This does not mean that the Blacks were better off than the Whites, but simply that they were more exploitable. They had been made exploitable, by conquest and subsequent legislation, to serve the interests of the White landowners; the mining companies traded on this position. Blacks could be exploited because they were already discriminated against; the mining industry further institutionalised this discrimination.

Racial discrimination is not in itself a productive activity and Whites have shown that the production of wealth for themselves is what they are primarily interested in. Now, however, the increasing focus of attention, both internally and internationally, on the injustice of racial discrimination, as well as the growing economic power and political awareness of Blacks, have made it necessary for the enlightened capitalists to move away from the practice of racial discrimination as the means of pursuing their own self-interest. To protect this same interest in a future non-racial society, more subtle forms of exploitation will have to be found.

Apologists for enlightened capitalism paint a different picture of the role played by racial discrimination in the past. They would have us believe that the intrusion of racial discrimination into the mining and other industries had nothing to do with industrial and economic factors, but was due entirely to the racism of the politicians and the White workers. They maintain that economic growth leads inevitably to the elimination of such injustices as racial discrimination and that economic growth, unimpeded by the imposition of racial discrimination for political reasons, would lead to economic and political freedom for everybody. This thesis, as Johnstone and others have shown, does not fit the historical facts, nor does it explain why racial discrimination was introduced in the first place. As Johnstone says,

> Given the vast economic growth and industrialisation which has taken place in South Africa during the twentieth century, and given the concomitant continuity and consolidation of the system of racial domination, it clearly makes little sense to begin by characterising the relationship between this system and the economic system as essentially 'dysfunctional'. [In other words, it *has* worked so you cannot start from the assumption that it *cannot* work. C.D.] Still less sense does this make in view of the extensive determination of the system of racial domination by property owners, notably in such forms of racial discrimination as the coercive labour controls of the contract system, the pass system and the compound system, and the various dscriminatory property laws. (*op.cit.,* p. 212).

Further, to say that racial discrimination was practised because people were racists is meaningless. It simply tells us something that we already know, namely, that racial discrimination exists; it does not tell us why. Such an 'answer' is as helpful as that of my two-year-old son who, when asked, 'Why do you wriggle?' replies, 'Because I'm a wriggler.' Racial discrimination *is* racism so it cannot be caused by it. To say that it is, is to say that people practise racial discrimination because they practise racial discrimination.

The inadequacy of this 'explanation' can be seen not only on the wider political level but also on the level of personal relationships. If Blacks were not a threat to the privileged economic position of Whites and if Whites did not need the labour of Blacks, there would be no cause of hostility or conflict. If Whites were nothing but demented racists, they would not want any contact at all with Blacks, but this would be of no benefit to them and so they do not do it. While they are not prepared to sit next to a Black on a bus they are quite happy to have far more intimate contact with Blacks by having them cook their food, look after their children, etc. They do not employ and underpay Blacks because they are Black but because they are exploitable. All sorts of myths about the needs, habits and cultural values of Blacks have been built up to 'justify' this position.

The creation of myths is not peculiar to South Africa or to the question of race; there used to be almost as many myths about the working class in England, for example, as there are now in South Africa about Blacks. Such myths are needed to provide an 'explanation' for actions which cannot be defended on rational and/or moral grounds. The capitalist value system provides some 'justification' for exploitation, but even that cannot justify the gross exploitation of Blacks. But since Whites benefit from and have become accustomed to exploiting Blacks, and since at the same time they claim to be rational beings, there must be some reason. They would not be able to do it to White people so, they conclude, there must be something different about Blacks. The breeding ground for such myths are the conditions which have been brought about by the practice which they are then used to 'explain'. The irrationality of this process is obvious. Thus, one argument for paying Blacks less than Whites is that their needs in respect of such items as housing, food and entertainment are less. The 'proof' of this myth lies in the fact that most Africans live in small houses, many live on little else but mealie meal, and they do not go to theatres. But all these things are the *result* of exploitation, they cannot also be a *reason* for it.

People came to believe these myths and this, compounded by ignorance, accounts for the performance of actions which can only be ascribed to race prejudice. Such myths are the counterpart on the personal level of the ideology of apartheid on the political level. On the political level there are some instances of racial discrimination which can only be described as the result of ideology gone mad; likewise, on the personal level, some of the most outrageous examples of racial discrimination are due to blind racial prejudice. In both cases the motivation is irrational, so the consequent behaviour does not fit into any rational analysis of the social system. This, of course, does not make it any less evil or lessen the need to prevent it. Such prejudice can be overcome and it is clearly very important that it should be. This, however, is not the main problem, because such prejudice is the consequence, not the cause, of a racially discriminatory system. Overcoming this prejudice will not eradicate the cause of hostility between racial groups.

Most opposition groups, however, particularly those of Christian inspiration, concentrate all their energies on this secondary factor of racial prejudice. This is partly because they accept the capitalist form of society as the normative one and the most obvious way in which South African society deviates from that norm is the racial nature of the forms of oppression; 'racism' is therefore presumed to provide the explanation for everything that is wrong with the system. It cannot be 'capitalism', because they start from the assumption that there is nothing wrong with capitalism; it can therefore only be 'racism'. That this does not, in fact, provide an explanation escapes their attention, because they also unquestioningly accept the capitalist analysis of the South African social system. But it is also a consequence of their 'idealist' understanding of truth, which as we have already seen, assumes that people's behaviour is determined by their knowledge or beliefs. This understanding leads them to be primarily concerned about people's mental *attitudes*. Since 'race' is the cause of the problem, and since behaviour is determined by attitudes, the whole problem is one of racial attitudes, the 'solution' is to persuade them to change these attitudes. The failure of this approach is not due to the hard-heartedness of the Nationalists, but to the fact that the cause of the problem is not in the Nationalists' or anybody else's 'hearts'. It cannot but fail because it is not concerned with the *cause* of the problem but only with its rationalisation.

Few but hardened Nationalists would deny that the present system in South Africa is an extremely oppressive one and that its most obvious feature is racial discrimination. However, to understand the nature and cause of this oppression it is not very helpful simply to describe the process; to overcome the oppression it is not sufficient simply to denounce it. The recording of the evils perpetuated by the Nationalist regime - the detention of people without trial, the wholesale removal of people, pass laws, etc. - is important for a number of reasons. But its use as 'ammunition' for moral denunciation is of very limited value in bringing about change. The problems that beset South Africa, and the injustices that are an integral part of the system, cannot be explained simply in terms of a racist ideology versus a capitalist or 'Christian' set of values and ideals.

To say that racial prejudice is a secondary factor does not mean that racial discrimination is secondary. Racial discrimination *is* 'the Problem'. The fact of racial discrimination is not in dispute; nor is the evilness of it. But that is not the question; the question is WHY?

The moralising attitude that this does not matter and that the main thing is that people are suffering under a system of racial discrimination and we must therefore change it, is not only naive; it also cannot lead to any effective action. I have seen enough of the misery and suffering caused by the present system not to wish in any way to play it down. But defining the problem is as elementarily necessary for its solution as is a doctor's diagnosing the cause of a sickness before attempting to cure it. It is not simply an academic question: it is an eminently practical one. I have not given an in-depth analysis, but I think I have said enough to show that racial discrimination is not an end in itself, but that its origin and development can only be explained by its relationship to the economic interests of Whites. At the very least, I hope it is sufficient to make some Christians question their acceptance of the capitalist norm and the capitalist analysis of the South African social system.

The obvious reason, therefore, for rejecting the enlightened capitalist option is that, since racial discrimination is not the cause of the problems of South African society, its elimination would not solve these problems; only the means of oppression would change. As long as the self-interest of one group, whatever the nature of the composition of that group, is its primary concern, it must oppress and exploit others. The enlightened capitalist 'solution', therefore, would not produce a social system essentially different from the present one. This is confirmed by their present practice and by the changes which they propose.

The change which is proposed to preserve White interests does not go any further in principle than the 'concessions' which the Nationalist government would be prepared to make in order to remain in power. The government is prepared to open certain facilities, for example five-star hotels and theatres, to all races, because their use is almost as restricted by money apartheid as it is by racial apartheid. The former restriction would continue to apply in an enlightened capitalist system. Government institutions are, in fact, ahead of many 'progressive' businessmen in actually narrowing the wage-gap. The Nationalists might even accept the principle of equal pay for equal work; though this principle is meaningless when the vast majority of Blacks do not have the opportunity of doing equal work. The enlightened capitalists might provide more such opportunities, but in order to humanise the conditions of workers it is not enough to pay a so-called 'just wage'.

Increasing wages, providing recreational facilities, introducing human relations techniques, are simply means, and often very effective ones, of diverting the workers' attention from the fact that they are being exploited. If they are happy at their work they are likely to be more productive; to be more efficient cogs in the machine. But they are still part of a machine, not people. This money can *only* be made by exploiting the workers. Where else can it come from? Money cannot of itself generate more money; it can only be turned into profits by labour.

Many capitalists may genuinely believe that they are very good to their 'labour' but if they are profiting from the fruits of that 'labour', which is what capitalism is all about, they are in fact exploiting people. They have become so efficient at doing this that many workers are not aware of their exploited condition. But a man has no more right to sell his labour than a woman has to sell her body. The one who puts a price of a man's labour or a woman's body, however, is the one who is responsible for dehumanising both himself and the worker/woman. The worker has been forced into this position and has been conditioned into accepting it. Increasing the price paid does not change the exploitative nature of the relationship. Man is meant to continue the work of creation and to transform the world by his labour. He must fulfil this role, and so fulfil himself both as a human being and as a Christian; *as* a worker, not despite being a worker. He cannot do this if his labour is a mere commodity which another man can buy and use in order to increase his own wealth.

In a capitalist system, no matter how well a worker might be treated, he is still an object, a production unit; his worth is measured in relation to the production process. He is a 'production-object' in much the same way as women are treated as 'sex-objects'. A man who pays a woman for her services is obviously exploiting her by using her as a 'sex-object'. This is not so obvious in the case of a man who ensconces his mistress in a luxury flat and smothers her with mink and diamonds; but he is still exploiting her if she is there only for the gratification of his own sexual desires. In South Africa Black workers have been placed in the position of prostitutes; the enlightened capitalists will 'elevate' them to the status of mistresses.

In a capitalist society there need only be a small minority who directly exploit others by appropriating to themselves the greater part of the product of other men's labour. The system relies for its support on those who share the same desire for wealth and who are prepared to use other people as stepping stones to acquire it. They are quite happy to be 'mistresses', provided they are sufficiently pampered; but the cost of their pampering must be paid for by others. In South Africa this cost has to be reckoned not only in terms of sweated labour, but also of lives lost. As song-writer David Marks wrote of the mine dumps in Johannesburg, 'You might think they are just mountains of dust. They're not. They're mountains of men.' No matter how 'generous' an individual capitalist might be, this cannot offset the fact that the money which he gives away, or the 'benefits' he provides for his workers, are the products of exploitation.

Capitalists like to claim that in a capitalist economic system everyone is free to compete on equal terms. Even accepting this as an ideal and leaving aside the moral consideration that it is not, because one can only compete at the expense of others, it is not true of any capitalist system. Success in a capitalist society owes more to inherited wealth and the opportunities this brings, than it does to hard work, intelligence or any human quality. The 'mistresses' are free to compete among themselves for favour, but the real capitalists are above this. This is particularly true in South Africa. Whites have monopolised wealth and power. To tell Blacks that they are now free to compete is not to give them an equal chance. If the enlightened capitalists were to gain political power, this would lead to the concentration of even more wealth in White hands and hence make Blacks even more exploitable. Presumably they would denationalise the State-owned corporations and hand them over to private enterprise. Thanks to the freedom bestowed by the capitalist system a Black labourer would then be free to compete with a White-owned R5000 million financial empire for the take over.

For Blacks to be free to compete with Whites, even on capitalist terms, it would be necessary for Whites to return what they have taken directly and indirectly from Blacks. They have shown no inclination to do this. Building schools for children whose fathers and grandfathers worked on the mines for 40 cents a shift until they died of lung disease can hardly be considered 'compensation'.

An oppressive society cannot be transformed into a human one by a wage increase. While this would make life a little easier for many people in South Africa, such improvements, which are all the enlightened capitalists have to offer, would do nothing to improve the quality of life of the vast majority. They could not do this because capitalism, enlightened or otherwise, is not concerned about the quality of life, except insofar as it thinks this can be bought. Capitalism, by definition, is concerned with profit; its sole criterion is material gain. Any concern which individuals might have for the spiritual is a purely private matter and has no influence on the capitalist system.

Capitalists, particularly those who also claim to be Christians, often condemn Marxism because it is 'materialist'; but in Marxism 'materialism' is opposed to 'idealism' and has nothing to do with concern for material things. It is capitalism which is 'materialist' in this sense. In the capitalist system not only the social status but the worth of a person is judged by what he has rather than by what he is. This values system has become so entrenched that even working-class people tend to accept its norms. A person 'has done well' if he owns his own house, has a large motor car, and earns a lot of money; what sort of person he is is secondary.

The most that could be achieved, therefore, by the enlightened capitalist 'solution' is some improvement in material conditions. While such needs as food and shelter are essential to man, they are only his animal needs. Providing for such needs should only be the starting point for a socio-political system, as it is in a socialist system; it should not be the most that people can hope for, as it is for the majority in a capitalist system.

The enlightened capitalists would also do away with such blatant injustices as detention without trial and that, of course, is to be welcomed. But such injustices are only 'necessary' in the present system because it is 'necessary' to exploit the majority of the population. As long as exploitation is a 'necessary' part of a system, means have to be devised to repress the aspirations of those who would threaten those who benefit from the exploitation. The enlightened capitalists might use less brutal means, but one cannot even be sure of that. After all, very 'enlightened' mining houses have no hesitation in calling in armed police to quell disturbances among their workers or in using vicious dogs to control them. The more subtle means that the capitalist system usually employs, however, can be even more dehumanising than brutal and obviously unjust ones; their subtlety does not lessen their evilness. I would certainly find it more dehumanising to be a wage-slave all my life than to be under house-arrest.

The 'acceptability' of their 'solution' to Blacks, which the enlightened capitalists like to claim, is no argument in its favour. In any event, it is based on very dubious grounds. Not all Blacks are as gullible as such people appear to think they are. I was told by a Black friend, who was very acceptable in 'liberal' circles, that he had attended hundreds of meetings with such people and had never once expressed his true views. Whites who took part in these meetings no doubt thought that they were having a meaningful exchange of opinion with an educated Black man and probably drew all sorts of conclusions from this about the views and aspirations of the Black man in general. He himself said, however, that every time he entered the meeting-room, which was invariably in a White-owned building in a White part of town, he became a different person. He needed these people's help, particularly financial, and therefore expressed views which would win their support. He then, in his own words, 'went back to the townships and had a good laugh with my chums about all the stupid things these Whites had said'. I am not generalising from one man's opinion and claiming that all or even most Blacks reject the enlightened capitalist solution; though there is plenty of evidence that many do. The only generalisation I am making is that not all Blacks are stupid and gullible.

In order to protect their economic interests, it is not necessary for the enlightened capitalists fully to control political power, as it is for the Nationalists. They are managing at present without doing this; though even in the present system they have some political power and considerable political influence. They must continue to have some power and they are endeavouring to ensure this in a society that is being forced to move away from racial discrimination. They are prepared to share a little of their wealth in order to gain the power which is needed for the protection of the rest of it. No doubt there are some Blacks who are prepared to sell their heritage and their brothers for a mess of pottage. The capitalist 'solution' does have its attractions; at least to the baser aspects of human nature. It leads to a very comfortable life for those on top. This top, which in the South African situation would continue to be predominantly White since they already control the wealth, needs to be supported by a very broad base which would continue to be almost exclusively Black. A slight change in the racial composition of these groups would do nothing to change the exploitative nature of the relationship between them.

While it is likely that change will move in the enlightened capitalist direction for some time - even with the Nationalists in power - there is little, if any, possibility of its being successful in the long term. Ultimately, the growing awareness of the root cause of their oppression by Blacks within South Africa, the pressure from neighbouring Black States, and the efforts of the external liberation movements will make it impossible for any White-dominated system, or even any capitalist system, to survive. This, however, is not a reason for Christians to reject this 'solution' (except perhaps for the Roman Catholic Church, which seems to have a knack of backing the winning side). Rather they should be positively working against it because of its fundamental incompatability with Christianity.

There can be no moral justification for Christians forming even a 'strategic alliance' with capitalism on the grounds that anything would be better than the present system.

> For, apart from any human aspects it may have picked up in its later developments, the basic ethos of capitalism is definitely anti-Christian: it is the maximising of economic gain, the idolising of the strong, the subordination of man to the economic production. Humanisation is for capitalism an unintended by-product, while it is for socialism an explicit good. Solidarity is for capitalism accidental; for socialism it is essential. In terms of their basic ethos, Christianity must criticise capitalism radically, in its fundamental intention, while it must criticise socialism functionally, in its failure to fulfil its purpose. (Bonino, *Marxists and Christians,* p. 115).

The argument about whether capitalism or socialism is more in keeping with Christian teaching cannot be resolved by either side trying to outdo the other in the number of Scriptural texts it can quote. Although those who would seek to justify capitalism, even on this level, would seem to face an impossible task. Capitalism is synonymous with the accumulation of wealth and this is clearly contrary to Christ's injunction not to 'store up treasures on earth'. It is not only the amount of wealth that a rich man has that makes it as impossible for him to enter the Kingdom of Heaven as it is for a camel to pass through the eye of a needle; it is also the fact that, in order to obtain this wealth within the essentially competitive capitalist system, he must make the pursuit of wealth his primary aim; he cannot therefore also 'Seek *first* the Kingdom of

Heaven'. To divide people into upper, middle and lower classes is obviously as un-Christian as dividing them into White, Coloured, Indian and African. Class, status, ancestry, education, talents, are as irrelevant to the Christian view of man as colour is.

Numerous other texts could be quoted to show that capitalist values are diametrically opposed to the New Testament norms. But the Bible, as I trust has been made clear in earlier chapters, is not meant to furnish 'proofs' or to define a political programme. It is meant to point out the direction which a Christian response to a particular situation should take. The general direction is towards the Kingdom of justice, peace, brotherhood and love which is to be inherited by the poor and the oppressed. As we saw in Chapter 2 these are not 'spiritual' values but political values which must be given historical form.

The decisive question for the Christian, therefore, is what political system can give effect to these values now, in a particular historical time and place. A Christian response cannot be arrived at from theological arguments alone, it is also necessary to 'read the signs of the times' (Vatican Council) and to understand the true nature of the political options available. A capitalist system cannot be an acceptable option, because it does not even set out to implement such values. 'Wealth', which dominates all capitalist thinking and practice, does not even feature among the values of the Kingdom. Capitalism, by definition, means the domination of the poor majority by the rich few; it cannot survive without dividing people into classes, without creating an elite. That this is true of capitalism in South Africa is clear from what we have seen of both its history and its present practice.

If it is so obvious that capitalism is incompatible with Christianity, why has the institutional Church always supported it, at least tacitly, and why are there so many Christians who are capitalists? Christianity and capitalism have been reconciled because, for historical reasons, it was considered to be in the interests of both to do so. Capitalism needed a 'private religion' and the professional dispensers of this private religion needed the financial and other support of the capitalists. I am not suggesting that this was done deliberately and maliciously. The analytical tools necessary for understanding the true nature of capitalism were not then available. The capitalist value system was therefore unquestioningly accepted as the norm. The Bible was then interpreted in the light of these values - there was nothing else in the light of which it could be understood; it cannot be understood purely objectively.

The 'Christianity' which resulted from such an interpretation could not be opposed to capitalism. It could not even question capitalism when its ready-made answers had already been determined by capitalism. It is no accident, for example, that the 'virtues' emphasised by such

'Christianity' - humility, honesty, thrift, hard work, obediance - are precisely the characteristics that an employer would look for in an employee. The 'God' of this 'Christianity' resembles a hard-bargaining captain of industry rather than a loving father of man. Man's relationship with God is seen in the essentially commercial terms which determine relationships in a capitalist society. Since you cannot run a business on love, it is assumed that God cannot run his business on that basis.

Any attempt to reconcile Christianity and capitalism can only be made within the framework of an 'idealist' understanding of Christian truth, which demands only an intellectual commitment to truth and an intellectual detachment from the evils of the world, not real, historical ones. This, as we have seen, is contrary to the biblical understanding of truth and of Christian practice, and is also sociologically and philosophically untenable - except for those in whose interest it is to hold on to it. If further proof is needed, try getting a person who is 'detached' from his wealth to part with it.

The analytical tools for exposing the true nature of capitalism and of a 'Christianity' which provided a 'moral' basis for it are now available, but Christians will only make use of them if they are prepared critically to examine their capitalist presuppositions. They cannot be persuaded by intellectual argument to do this. For as Ruben Alves says: 'Our ability to understand does not go beyond the limits of our experience. Very few words are needed when we have eaten of the same bread, and a multiplicity of words is of no avail if we have not felt common sufferings and hopes.' (*op.cit.,* p. 182).

The experience of White South African Christians is of the wealth and comfort that capitalism provides for the 'privileged' few, so they are not likely to question it. Church leaders, who tend to move in the same social circles as capitalists and to rely on their patronage, cannot be expected to challenge this acceptance of the capitalist *status quo.* (After all, how can a man who gives R50,000 for the building of a church be part of an un-Christian system?) But fortunately, we do not have to wait for them. 'The past has shown,' as Schillebeeckx has pointed out, 'that, long before the Churches had analyzed the social problems, there were people who, in their commitment and in a pre-analytic dialogue with the world, had already reached the moral decision that fundamental changes were required. New situational ethical imperatives have rarely or never been initiated by philosophers, theologians, Churches or ecclesiastical authorities. They emerge from a concrete experience of life and impose themselves with the clear evidence of experience.' (*God the Future of Man,* p. 153).

Many White Christians might not even be convinced by the experience of a socialist system as a reality in South Africa. But the fact that vast numbers of Church members, both in South Africa and throughout the world, reject the Church's alliance with capitalism, should at least make Church leaders question their own blind acceptance of it. The task of the Church is to reflect upon the experience of its members and only then to take its stand. The experience of the vast majority of its members is of poverty and oppression; many of these have decided that their condition cannot be improved under a capitalist system. If the Church is, as it claims to be, the Church of the poor and is continuing the work of Christ who came 'to preach the good news to the poor . . . to set the down-trodden free', it is to the experience of this majority that it must give its attention. It is not sufficient to declare its support verbally; it must actually follow the lead given by them and this entails, among other things, the rejection of capitalism.

This is not to say that truth is arrived at by means of a Gallup poll. We have seen that the incompatibility of capitalism and Christianity can be demonstrated, but that alone is not sufficient to remove the 'block' that people who have always accepted capitalism have against even considering the possibility that it could be wrong. The actual rejection of capitalism by an increasing number of Christians should serve to awaken their capitalist brethren to the existence of this possibility. They could then at least bring a critical awareness, instead of an unquestioned acceptance, of their capitalist presuppositions to their consideration of the evidence.

The traditional Christian, particularly Roman Catholic, complete rejection of communism led one to believe that every individual communist had at least one cloven hoof. By my equally complete rejection of the capitalist system I do not imply that all capitalists are ogres. There are many good people who are capitalists, including many who would be considered by churchpeople to be good Christians. There are, however, equally good people who are Nationalists and whose zeal for upholding 'Christian' values is matched only by the ardour of their support for apartheid. John Vorster is doubtless a loving father and a doting grandfather; he is also ultimately responsible for a situation where three children die from malnutrition every hour of the day. As a politician it is on the latter fact that he must be judged. Likewise, capitalists are to be judged on the system they uphold, not on their personal character. Criticism is aimed at the system, not at individuals who might be in completely good faith and for whom change might be beyond their present capability. I personally have benefited from the generosity of such people and am duly grateful for this; there are some for whom I have the greatest respect. But this does not, and must not, prevent me from believing that the system which they uphold is totally incompatible with Christianity.

Even if churchpeople cannot yet see the basic contradiction between capitalism and Christianity, they should at least be able to realise that in the South African situation the enlightened capitalist approach cannot lead to a society in which the human dignity of each person is fully recognised. If the Church continues its present support for this approach, not only will it be supporting an immoral, un-Christian system, but its opposition to the present regime will not go beyond moralising about its blatant injustices. It will be satisfied with a system, any system, which eliminates these. The Church in South Africa will then, instead of having its own peculiar irrelevancy, simply be as irrelevant as the Church in Europe. Perhaps that is all it aspires to. If so, not only will it die, it will deserve to die, because it is not keeping alive the hope of the fulfilment of Christ's promise.

The enlightened capitalist 'solution', therefore, is to be rejected, because it is no solution. It does not set out to tackle the root cause of the evils of the present system and proposes an alternative which is not essentially different from the Nationalist system. While the attempt to eliminate racism is to be welcomed, capitalism, for which racism is primarily a disguise, is in itself, in its end and in the means it uses to achieve that end, completely irreconcilable with Christianity. Not only can Christians not support efforts directed towards this 'solution', they must positively oppose them, since they can only delay the establishment of a free, genuinely human society. In opposing such efforts one is also opposing the Nationalist system, because both 'solutions' rely ultimately on the control of political and economic power by a minority. The only alternative to both is a politico-economic system in which all share equally.

chapter 8
A Socialist Option

Private property does not constitute for anyone an absolute and
unconditioned right. No one is justified in keeping for his exclusive
use what he does not need, when others lack necessities . . . some
opinions have arisen in human society - we do not know how - that
considered profit as the most important incentive to encourage
economic progress, free competition as the supreme form of
economics, and private ownership of the means of production as an
absolute right which would not accept limits or a corresponding
social obligation. One cannot condemn such abuses too strongly by
solemnly recalling once again that the economy is at the service of
man . . . What must be aimed at is complete humanism. And what is
that if not the fully-rounded development of the whole man and of
all men?

These are not the words of some radical 'political priest', but of Pope
Paul VI in his encyclical letter *'Populorum progressio'*. I do not know
whether the Pope was aware of it, but 'development of the whole man
and of all men' is the economist Perroux's definition of socialism.

Pope Paul's statement is an indication that the Roman Catholic
Church realises that it over-reacted to the rise of socialism. For some
time the Roman Church, in common with others, was a staunch
defender of the right to the private ownership of property. No attempt
was made, however, to reconcile this right with the whole Old Testament
tradition of the divine ownership of land and the obligation of everybody,
as God's tenant, to offer the first fruits to Him, or with the New
Testament condemnation of the rich; or with the early Christian
communalism; or with the teaching of the Fathers of the Church who
maintained that 'All possessions are sins' and 'You are not making a gift
of your possessions to the poor person. You are handing over to him
what is his. For what has been given in common for the use of all, you
have arrogated to yourself. The world is given to all, not only to the
rich.' (St Ambrose); 'All riches come from injustice. Unless one person
has lost another cannot find. Therefore I believe that the popular

proverb is very true: "The rich man is either an unjust person or the heir of one." ' (St Jerome).

Owing to the particular paranoia that South Africans have about 'communism', it is perhaps necessary to state at the outset what I do *not* mean by socialism: I do not mean Soviet socialism, or as it is more usually called, 'Russian communism'. Soviet socialism is an excessively dogmatic and economistic interpretation of socialism, which has led to bureaucratic rather than people's control of the means of production, and to the formation of its own privileged class. The needs of the people have been subordinated to the needs of a distortion of the ideology which was intended to meet these needs. Socialism can be distorted as easily as Christianity can. I doubt whether any Christian who is a socialist would defend Soviet practice; neither would many non-Christian Marxists. On the other hand, as Bonino warns,

> Christians should be careful before indulging in self-righteous denunciation of 'Stalinist terror' and 'communist oppression' without realising that at least as much terror and oppression - often even without hope - is abroad in the Western world under the pretence of defending 'Christian values' and 'the Christian way of life'. Nothing that a horrified European bourgeois can read about Soviet terror in Solzhenitsyn's *Gulag Archipelago* is new to the subjects of the 'most Christian' governments of Brazil, Uruguay or Chile.' (*Christians and Marxists,* p. 87).

Or to Black South Africans?

A Christian must judge a political system, not by the capitalist criteria of efficiency, productivity, and the opportunities provided for personal gain, but by its effectiveness in giving historical form to the values of the Kingdom: peace, justice, equality, freedom and love. These values cannot be realised in a capitalist system, because the accumulation of wealth and the consequent conflict of interests is, by definition, an integral part of any capitalist system. We, therefore, have to look to some form of socialism.

This is not to say that socialism is a negative choice, which we only opt for because of the default of capitalism. Socialism is a reaction against capitalism, but since it is the negation of the evils of capitalism it is a positive system. On the other hand, it is not necessary, or possible, to claim that it is the best of all possible systems; all that can be demanded is that it be the better of the two now available. We cannot give practical expression to our beliefs, in our present historical situation, by means of a political system which has either ceased to exist or does not yet exist. Nor is it possible to find a middle 'Christian' way between capitalism and socialism. Christianity is not a political system. It does not have the political institutions which are necessary in modern society for ordering the complex interrelationships between people and between countries. Neither does it have its own method of analysis, which is necessary to determine the true nature of a given historical situation. As we have noted, attempts to make a 'Christian' contribution in South Africa usually presuppose a capitalist understanding of our society. The Gospels can no more tell us how to organise a particular society than they can tell us how to perform an open-heart operation. They tell us what society should be like, but they do not tell us how to bring it about. I can say as a Christian that capitalism is immoral, but Christianity tells me nothing about the actual mechanics of, for example, dismantling a vast financial empire and disposing of the wealth for the benefit of the whole of society. But it is part of my Christian responsibility to find the best way of doing this; simply holding the intellectual conviction that capitalism is immoral does not constitute a Christian response. If we are to oppose capitalism, which as Christians we must, we need to have an alternative politico-economic system, which only socialism provides.

'The development of the whole man and of all men', to which Pope Paul referred, can only take place within a socialist system, because it is only within such a system that man is accorded the freedom and responsibility which are his God-given right. To quote Pope Paul again: 'The Bible, from the first page on, teaches that the whole creation is for man, that it is his responsibility to develop it by intelligent effort and by means of his labour to perfect it, so to speak, for his own use. If the world is made to furnish each individual with the means of livelihood and the instruments for his growth and progress, each man has therefore the right to find in the world what is necessary for himself.' In a capitalist system, this responsibility, which belongs to all men, as men - not as rich, or educated, or White or any other sub-section of mankind - is arrogated to the few who have effective power. Arrogance, like selfishness, is an endemic vice of capitalism; capitalists claim sole agency rights over God's creation.

Man exercises his responsibility for creation primarily by using 'his labour to perfect it'. He cannot do this in a capitalist society, because his labour is no longer his; he is forced to sell it, and thus to sell part of himself, to another man. Both man and his labour are turned into objects which can be evaluated in terms of money. Man can only responsibly exercise his God-given domination over creation and over his own labour - and thus be fully human - if he has direct control over what he produces, how he produces it and the use to which the product of his labour is put; in other words, if workers themselves own and control the means of production.

To claim that people are not capable of doing this is to deny either their humanity or God's purpose in creating man. People are quite capable of being people, but the capitalist system does not allow them to be. It is true that in 'developed' capitalist societies the dehumanising nature of the work situation is not so obvious as it once was; but it is also true, firstly, that any improvements that have been made have been wrung from the capitalists by the militancy of the workers, and, secondly, that being human involves much more than having one's fill of 'bread and circuses'. Capitalism might achieve a rising standard of living, but only at the cost of a 'falling standard of life'. And even the standard of living can only be maintained at the expense of the continued exploitation of the Third World.

Paternalistic 'charity', which is all that capitalism can offer, is no substitute for the recognition of man's freedom, responsibility and dignity in his working and all other relationships. Working relationships are of primary importance not only because people spend a large proportion of their time in their work situation, but also because these determine to a great extent how people live the rest of their lives. In the capitalist system, money, as the determinant of status and as the means of evaluating people and things, becomes the intermediary of virtually every relationship and hence dehumanises them; money takes the place of any giving of oneself.

On the other hand, for both socialism and Christianity, the bond between men is their common humanity.

> The Marxist and Christian view of man emphatically states, to start with, that man is a social creature. Man is not an abstract, isolated creature content in himself. He lives in association with others. He is a social being. That is the fundamental qualification of his existence, and that is his delimitation of his being as a man. He has to be in actual solidarity with other men, not bound up in concern for his own individuality only. That is the way of human fulfilment in a personal and social sense. Above all, that solidarity means fellowship with the poor and oppressed, the weary and heavyladen. (J.M. Lochman, *Church in a Marxist Society*).

Socialism provides the structures necessary for such solidarity and fellowship; whereas capitalism divides society and sees other people as a threat, as competitors. Christianity gives an added meaning to this solidarity and fellowship, but it does not have its own political structures which are necessary for putting them into effect. The concern for truly human relationships might be dismissed by capitalists as 'sickly

There are various forms of socialism, which of its nature must take different forms in different historical contexts, but all have a common *aim:* the creation of an egalitarian society, free from the inherent class conflicts of capitalism, in order to further 'the development of the whole man and of all men'. I have never heard of any theological argument against this aim. Even the definition of communism given by the Communist Party of the Soviet Union seems to me to be beyond reproach from a Christian point of view:

> Communism is a classless social system with one form of public ownership of the means of production and full social equality of all members of society; under it, the all-round development of people will be accompanied by the growth of the productive forces through continuous progress in science and technology; all sources of public wealth will gush forth abundantly, and the great principle 'from each according to his ability to each according to his needs' will be implemented. Communism is a highly organised society of free socially-conscious working people in which public self-government will be established, a society in which labour for the good of society will become the prime vital requirement of everyone, a necessity recognised by one and all, and the ability of each person will be employed to the greatest benefit of the people.

Those who believe that 'there is no such thing as Jew and Greek, slave and freeman, male and female; for you are all one person in Jesus Christ' (*Gal.,* 3.28), can hardly object to a classless society where there is full social equality. If *the* mark of a Christian is his love for others, how can he object to the creation of a society where 'labour for the good of society will be the prime vital requirement'?

The primary and essential *means* that socialism employs in order to achieve this aim, namely, the public ownership and control of the means of production, likewise cannot be objected to on theological grounds. Socialists do not wish to take over the control of the means of production in order to punish the rich, private owners (Marx himself insisted that socialism was also for the good of the capitalists); nor simply to ensure that workers are better paid. Socialism is much more than an alternative economic system to capitalism. It is concerned with the whole man; and it recognises that part of man's wholeness is his relationship with others. His relationship with others in society, however, is primarily determined by the method of production in that society. If the means of production are privately owned, the mode of production and the consequent form of society will be ordered to the benefit of the few owners. If all are to benefit from what they produce and to have an equal place in society, all must share in the ownership of the means of production. This is not a dogma of socialism or of Marxism particularly; it is a conclusion drawn from the historical observation of how societies have functioned. Even the brief mention we have made of some aspects of South African history is sufficient to show the validity of this conclusion in the South African historical context: the nature of society, including the form and extent of racial discrimination, changed with the change from a land-based economy to a mining and industrialised one.

Private owners of the means of production are not simply richer than the workers; because they are richer, they also have more power; directly over the worker and the product of his labour and indirectly over the whole of society. Although in a democratic capitalist system each person may have one vote and so theoretically be politically equal, in fact it is the rich who have the money, leisure, and education to organise and manipulate political forces. It is the rich, particularly through their control of the Press and other media and their influence on the educational structures, who set the standards for society. They decide that productivity, efficiency, wealth, etc. are the primary values, then everybody is judged in the light of these values. But these 'values' are determined by their ownership of the means of production. The public ownership of the means of production, therefore, is not an ideological end in itself; it is the necessary means of bringing about a better society which is not determined by the material interests of a few members of society.

The interpretation and practice of Christianity has become so bound up with capitalism that when Christians oppose socialism they imagine they are objecting on Christian grounds; in fact all they are saying is that socialism is not capitalism. Private ownership, the cult of individualism (which is not the same as concern for every individual person), competitiveness, are capitalist values, not Christian values. On the other hand, concern for others is *the* basic Christian value; and socialism provides the means for giving practical effect to this concern.

The most common criticism of socialism, by Christians and non-Christians alike, is that it limits individual freedom. Firstly, 'individual freedom' in this context is no more than a euphemism for selfishness. Capitalism has succeeded in making a virtue out of what for the Christian is the fundamental vice: 'Each man for himself.' Further, a person's individual freedom is limited in any society by the rights of others. It is obvious that the workers are not free in a capitalist society. They have no control over their labour or the product of their labour; and they are further limited by the lack of money in a society where money is god. But the freedom of the capitalist too is limited by the means which other people use to make money. The only freedom that socialism removes is the freedom to exploit others. It regulates the freedom of all in the interests of the freedom of all.

There is no need to create political and social structures to safeguard man's concern for himself; that is one thing that all men can be relied upon to do. In saying that 'you must love your neighbour *as yourself'*, Christ was not saying that you must love yourself first in order to be able to love your neighbour; he assumed that people did love themselves, he did not have to command them to do so. It is not love of self that is the mark of Christ's disciples or the measure of their love of God. A man can love himself and claim to love God, but he is still a liar if he does not love his brother.

Concern for individual freedom only arises in a society where material gain is the ideal, and this ideal can only be attained at the expense of others. It has nothing to do with Christianity, which is concerned with forming mankind into a community because the common destiny of mankind is *sharing* in one Kingdom. Neither Christianity nor socialism says that society is *more important than* the individual. They both say that man is essentially *part* of society and that his social relationships are part of him. It is only possible, therefore, to be concerned about individual people by being concerned about society. A person only needs to try to emphasise his separateness from, and independence of, society when he considers society, that is, other people, to be a threat to him; as is the case in a capitalist society. A capitalist must defend the 'rights of the individual' over against 'society' because he can only realise his ideal - material profit - at the expense of other people. 'Individualism' springs from, and is necessary for, capitalism, *not* Christianity. We cannot live, nor can we be saved, as individuals, our 'social-ness' is an essential part of our humanness and of our Christianness.

Another criticism of socialism is that it takes away the motivation for personal initiative. Because capitalists themselves are motivated by the desire for personal material gain, it does not follow that this can be the only motivation for all men. Personal satisfaction, self-fulfilment, service to others are nobler and just as effective motivations. Further, once people understand that their own interests are intimately bound up with the interests of everybody in society, they will realise that they are not working for some abstract entity called 'society', but for themselves. If society prospers, not only materially but also by becoming more human, they too will prosper. The purpose in life for a Christian, as well as for everybody else, is to become fully human and this cannot be measured according to the capitalist norms of 'success'.

Any form of socialism which is not to remain a dream or, in practice, is not to develop into a thinly-disguised form of State capitalism with a few welfare services thrown in, must at least take account of Marxist theory and analysis, since it was Marx who provided the scientific foundation which enables socialism to be implemented. Both space and the limits of my own knowledge preclude any detailed critique of Marxism and its compatibility with Christianity. While it is necessary, for both Marxism and Christianity, that there should be 'dialogue' on a theoretical level - as has been taking place in Europe and America for many years and is now taking place in some socialist countries - this is not the immediate concern of those who are involved in a struggle for liberation; and everybody in South Africa is involved in such a struggle on one side or the other, whether we like it or not. Neither Marxism nor Christianity is an abstract theory. Both are concerned with praxis: the theory is a reflection of, and is reflected in, action and cannot in fact be separated from it. Few, if any, people become Marxists because they are captivated by the intellectual beauty and coherence of dialectical materialism; rather, they see Marxism as an effective method of changing an unjust and oppressive social system. Likewise, few people become Christians or members of a particular Church because of the weight of the intellectual arguments offered. In my own experience, the fact of who visited a person when he/she was sick had more to do with whether that person became a Zionist or Roman Catholic than did their respective doctrines. The task of the Christian is to make his love for his neighbour real and effective in his own particular historical situation. The most important question, therefore, is whether Marxism can help him do this.

More and more Christians, in South Africa as well as in other parts of the world, are deciding that it can; in some places it has shown that it can. There are, for example, more hungry people in the so-called free world than there are in socialist countries; 'the starving millions in China' are no longer a byword; only socialist countries were prepared to help Angola and Mozambique in their fight for independence. On a different level, among White South Africans, although there have been some outstanding Christians, 'communists' have, generally speaking, shown a far greater commitment to bringing about radical change than Christians have; and, of course, the exceptional Christians have usually been labelled 'communist'. While for moral and/or political reasons, one might not approve of all that they have done, one cannot but admire the depth of commitment involved in being prepared to risk one's life for what one believes in.

The task of theology is to reflect on such facts; not to try to impose preconceived ideas of a 'Christian' solution. Theology must reflect on the failure of capitalism, to which institutionalised Christianity has been allied, and the practical claims and successes of socialism. And this not, on the one hand, because Christians want to outdo socialists, nor, on the other, because we believe that 'if you can't beat 'em, join 'em'. But because socialism sets out to do what we as Christians want to do, namely, to transform the world, and perhaps we can learn something from it about how to do this.

Capitalists would argue that socialism has in fact failed and would claim that all socialist countries are poor because they are socialists; other criticisms of socialist practice usually refer only to the specific form this has taken in the Soviet Union. Regarding the general argument, President Nyerere makes three points:

> The first is that to measure a country's wealth by its Gross National Product is to measure things, not satisfactions . . . the spread of good health through the eradication of endemic diseases may, or may not, be recorded as an increase in statistical national wealth, it is certainly better for people if it has happened. My second point is that a successful harlot, or a favoured slave, may be better off materially than a woman who refuses to sell her body, or a man to sell his freedom. We do not regard the condition of the harlot or slave as being consequently enviable . . . Thirdly, I do not accept that the socalled unworkability of socialism has been proved. Capitalism has been developing for about two centuries. The first national commitment to socialism was made in 1917, by a backward and feudal nation devastated by war, which has subsequently suffered greatly from further civil and international conflict. Even so, few people would deny the material transformation which has been effected in the U.S.S.R. during the past fifty five years. And in fact, despite the major criticisms which can be made of all the socialist countries, it is difficult to argue that their people are worse off than the late capitalist starters - countries like Greece, or Spain or Turkey, for example. On the contrary, they are clearly better off in the vital matters of health, education and the security of their food and shelter. Whether or not they have the same number of television sets seems to me much less important. (Address delivered at Sudanese Socialist Union Headquarters, Khartoum, 1973; reprinted in *New Blackfriars,* Oct. 1974).

Obviously socialism has failed - if it is judged by capitalist norms. It has also failed to some extent on socialist terms, particularly because socialism is not solely concerned with material prosperity. But socialism is not a perfect system, nor is it implemented by perfect people. The fact that some of the evils that are present in capitalist society, such as selfishness and the desire for personal material gain, persist even in a socialist society shows, I think, that not *all* the evils of society derive from man's relationship to the means of production. Christianity has a more comprehensive 'theory' on man's tendency to evil than Marxism does; we believe that all men are sinners; this fact is manifested in political and social structures, but also in individual people.

The question of practical co-operation between Christians and Marxists is not the present concern of the White Christians in South Africa; though it might well be in the future. However, the need for the use of Marxist theory and analysis has already arisen. On this level there is no real problem for a Christian.

> It is possible . . . to consider Marxism exclusively as a set of analytic tools concerning economic activity and its political and social significance. Such tools make it possible to analyse capitalist society and bourgeois culture in a dynamic way and therefore to project a political strategy of change. It is even possible in this respect to receive the Marxist criticism of religion . . . as a valid instrument for understanding and criticising bourgeois Christianity, and therefore as a valuable contribution to a true renewal of the churches. This rather instrumental understanding of Marxism has not only been accepted by some Christians but also by many revolutionaries and political leaders in the Third World, who would not declare themselves Marxists but would freely recognise that their programme and policies are deeply indebted to Marxist theory and analysis. In this respect one may go further and say that Marxist insights, like any other scientific discovery, are now a generally available resource and, as such, it is not only legitimate for the Christian to use it, but he is morally obligated to do so to the extent that it proves to be scientifically accurate and valuable. (Bonino, *op.cit.,* p. 121).

On this level, the philosophical foundations and total world view of Marxism are as irrelevant as are those of the mechanic who fixes one's car. The use of Marxist methodology does not make one a Marxist; particularly in the eyes of Marxists. From what I have said in the two previous chapters, I think it is obvious and essential that Christians as well as everybody else make use of Marxist 'analytical tools' in order to get to the root of the problems of South African society. Whether one can go further is largely an academic question in South Africa at present. This does not mean that it should not be pursued; only that there is no need to go into it here.

However, for many Christians any contact at all with Marxism is completely anathema because of its atheistic, materialistic, and antireligious, in particular,anti-Christian, character. The part that these factors play in Marxism depends on the interpretation given to them in the various forms of Marxism. They only raise problems for Christians, and some would say also for Marxists, when they are made absolute. A Christian cannot accept that Marxism is a *total explanation* of man and of history; he can accept it as a *scientific description.* Marxism can explain what happens in society and how it happens; it cannot *fully* explain, for a Christian, why it happens. All this really means is that a Christian cannot make a religion out of Marxism; but neither can he make an ideology out of Christianity.

Christians have as much right to criticise Marxists as Marxists have to criticise Christians; and each should welcome the criticism of the other. Since Christian practice has to a large extend been formed in and by capitalist society, capitalism does not present any challenge to this practice. Marxism, however, arose, partially at least, as a reaction against bourgeois 'Christianity' and hence does present such a challenge.

> A Christian, when confronted with this challenge, should not hasten to refute it, but should rather ask himself how can he understand it, what is it that he is being told about himself and his community. As Christians we are not judged by Marx or Marxism; one alone is our judge: the Lord. But Marx is a witness. And he witnesses against us precisely at those points where we have received a very definite responsibility: love, justice, abundant life for all men, the responsibility for creation and the world, the care of the poor. We must try to understand his accusation. (Bonino, *Christians and Marxists,* p. 58).

I suspect that many Christians who condemn Marxism for being *materialist* have not taken the trouble to understand what is meant by this. In so far as 'materialism' refers to an understanding of history which is opposed to an 'idealist' understanding, Christianity is not threatened by it. Christianity has been interpreted in purely idealist terms and this, as we have seen, has led to a perverted and unbiblical understanding of Christianity. Christianity is not a body of abstract truths; it is a practical response, the nature of which is determined in and by a particular historical situation. This response can and must be explained in materialist terms. A materialist understanding of history therefore plays an important part in determining a true and effective Christian practice; it cannot, however, be accepted as a total, all-embracing, exclusive understanding of reality. Like the German theologian, Dorothee Solls, we should 'rebel against the spiritualisation or dematerialisation of faith in theology, in which it would be possible to understand Calvary without Vietnam, Chile or Dimbaza. Faith, hope and love should not be spiritualised and divorced from concrete situations.' (*South African Outlook,* Sept. 1974).

A materialist philosophy cannot be primarily interested in the truth or falsity of beliefs in immaterial entities; 'from the fact that you can explain *why* a certain belief is held by a group of people in terms of the material conditions of their social relationships, it does not follow that the proposition they believe in is *false.*' (D. Turner, *New Blackfriars,* June 1975). One may have reservations about whether material conditions *alone* determine beliefs, but even allowing that they do, this does not account for their truth or falsity. Marxism, as a materialist philosophy, is primarily interested in whether the praxis, of which such beliefs form a part, leads to the emancipation or to the alienation of man.

There can be little doubt that the Christian practice that was prevalent at the time of Marx was bound to be, and deserved to be, rejected by anyone who was as passionately concerned as Marx was about the freedom and dignity of man. Marxism is not in fact *atheistic* in the biblical understanding of the word. According to the Bible, the one who does not know God is he who does not do justice or who does not love his brother. The Marxist denial of God is a rejection of the 'idealist' profession of belief in God; if this denial is made into a dogma, it is itself an idealist response. But Christianity, as an historical response to God, is not primarily concerned with such professions or denials.

Atheism is only 'necessary' for Marxism in so far as concern for God detracts from concern for man. The God of the Greeks, the God of liberal capitalism *is* opposed to the full emancipation of man; the God of the Bible, the God of Jesus Christ is not and has shown that He is not. Marx could not have rejected this God, because he did not know Him; He had been confined by Christians to another world.

When the proletariat opened its eyes a hundred years ago and awakened to self-consciousness, it is not true that Christ was arrogantly rejected; it would be much truer to say that in a sense, Christ was not there at all. Christ was invisible and inaudible. When the old Christian order of life for the peasantry and the people of the small towns was no longer viable for the proletarian, because he had been lifted out of this order into a completely different strange order, Christ should have been made visible to him in a new way through the mediation of 'Christians' . . . This did not happen. No Christian of stature at that point broke through the barrier between middle class, the peasant class and the feudal class. And so Christ remained invisible . . . Let us be pitilessly clear on this point: this is how 'Marxism' came into existence. The Marxists fell into error but the greater part of the blame lay with Christians. The recognition of this fact must strike a deadly blow at the root of all Christian self-satisfaction in relation to Marxism. The burden of proletariat unbelief lies on our shoulders. This unbelief does not separate us from these men, it actually binds us to them. (Walter Dirks, quoted in H. Gollwitzer, *The Christian Faith and the Marxist Criticism of Religion,* pp. 91-2).

Many Marxists would claim that atheism and the rejection of Christianity are absolutely essential to Marxism. In doing so, however, they do not seem to be consistent with their own historical materialism. On the basis of such a philosophy it is not possible to make *any* absolute statement. The teachings of Marx, and even less so of Lenin, cannot be the last word for Marxists. Neither Marx nor anybody else can say that Christianity, *as such,* alienates man from himself, because Christianity *as such* does not exist; it takes a different form in different historical contexts. Likewise, Marxism too does not exist as such, so its atheism, 'however absolutely it may be formulated as allegedly timeless truth, belongs all the same to the historically-conditioned ideology of the movement, conditioned by the mental, social and political climate of the time of its origin, by the development of the relation between faith and science, by its experience from time to time in relation to religious groups' (Gollwitzer, *op.cit.,* pp. 102-3).

Unfortunately, present-day Christian practice is not really much of an improvement on that of Marx's time, so Marxists do have some reason for being, in practice, militantly *anti-Christian.* The functional basis of this practice is presently being illustrated by the harmonious relationships between Christians and Marxists in South America. (It will be interesting to see whether it is borne out by Marxism being less virulently anti-Christian in Rhodesia, where the Church has made an effort to identify with the cause of the oppressed, than it is in Mozambique, where the Church, with a few exceptions like the White Fathers, did not.) It is also true, however, that Marxism has been turned by some into a substitute religion. Even though the 'God' who has been rejected had been used as a 'stop gap', the removal of the stop has still left a gap, which has been filled by accepting Marxism, with religious fervour, as a total world-view.

The Christian response to Marxism, therefore, should not be, on the one hand, a complete rejection of it as the work of the anti-Christ, nor, on the other, an unquestioning, uncritical acceptance of it. The Christian response should be to examine our own practice in the light of the criticisms that Marxism offers. We should do this not in order to ingratiate ourselves with Marxists nor in order to justify ourselves to them or to anybody else, but in order, literally, to justify our own existence as Christians. Church leaders, in particular, must at least question whether their pathological antipathy towards Marxism derives from their own ingrained capitalism and their fear of government action being taken against them or from an as objective as possible study of Marxism in the light of the Scriptures. Marxism denies the existence of a 'God' who never existed and rejects a travesty of Christianity. Christians should be more concerned about the practical atheism of capitalism, which by its inherent injustice denies the existence of the living God and makes a substitute god of money. The Marxist critique helps us to expose the domestication and emasculation that Christianity has undergone in the service of capitalism.

I am not suggesting that Christians should become rabid Marxists; I would certainly not describe myself in those terms. Since I am writing specifically for Christians, I am concerned with what Marxism or socialism has to offer Christians and not with what Christianity has to offer Marxists or socialists. But because of the common aims of socialism and Christianity, on the one hand, and the ineffectiveness and total moral unacceptability of the 'enlightened capitalist solution' on the other, it is essential for Christians to opt for socialism. For this socialism to be realistic and effective it must incorporate the use of the 'analytic tools' of Marxism. As Christians, we are obliged to seek to understand the true nature of the problems of our society and only a socialist analysis is able to pierce the smokescreen of Nationalist propaganda and to expose the veiled self-interest of the 'enlightened capitalists'. To reject the socialist alternative is to take the side of the capitalists, and, indirectly, of the Nationalists.

The primary political task of the Christian in South Africa is to oppose and ultimately to replace the present system. The ineffectiveness of the present opposition, of Christians and others, is due largely to a lack of understanding of the true nature of the problem, and to the failure to see the possibility and desirability of a radical alternative; another factor, of course, is the brutal efficiency of the repressive measures taken by the Nationalists. All I have attempted to show is, firstly, only socialism provides the basis for an effective opposition, and secondly, socialism is the only morally acceptable alternative for a Christian.

The 'theoretical' exposition of the precise nature of the political, economic, and social institutions that are necessary for the implementation of socialism is the work of experts in these fields, and this work must be judged by scientific norms; there are no specifically Christian ones. (Such 'theorising' cannot, of course, be done by experts in isolation, but only in interaction with those who are actively involved in the process of liberating themselves.) A Christian is concerned about the creation of a society in which the freedom, dignity, equality and responsibility of each person is recognised in practice; he has no particular competence as a Christian to decide on the best means of achieving this. This does not mean that he has to suspend any moral judgement on the means used, but that the political efficacy of these means is *part of* his moral judgement. A Christian can only express the political involvement that is demanded of him as a Christian by being a socialist; but there is no separate Christian way of being a socialist. The relationship between Christianity and socialism in this respect is no different from the relationship between Christianity and any other science. If, for example, a person is a Christian and a doctor, the better Christian he is the more conscientious a doctor he will be and the more conscientious a doctor he is the better Christian he will be, but his being a Christian does not change the nature of his 'doctorness'; *qua* doctor he can only be judged by medical standards. If you want to know whether a doctor is a good doctor you do not ask his parish priest, you ask his colleagues, or better still, his patients. Mending a broken leg is a good and Christian thing to do, but there is no Christian method of doing it. Likewise, there is no Christian method of achieving the good and Christian aims of socialism. Bishops and priests, therefore, are not necessarily the best people to decide how this should be achieved; nor am I competent to do so in any detail.

Possibly the most important thing that Whites, Christians or otherwise, can do for the realisation of a socialist society in South Africa is to stop either bolstering up the present system or seeking to replace it with another form of capitalism. Both activities involve the imposition of a preconceived and foreign system on Blacks. White domination was imposed by conquest and is maintained by force; the 'enlightened capitalists' seek to impose their system by money, by buying Blacks into it. The suggestion by some capitalists that the unique solution for South Africa lies in the wedding of African 'ubuntu' to capitalist expertise is racist and grossly paternalistic. In effect they are saying to Africans: 'You are very nice people, but actually you are too stupid to cope with the modern world. Let us take you by the hand and show you the way. You don't have to thank us; just sing a song or do a dance.'

Socialism, however, does not seek to impose anything on anyone. It offers to oppressed people the means of arriving at a critical understanding of, and of changing, their situation. It can only be implemented when people are conscious of the need for it and are willing to make sacrifices for it. But every historical situation is unique; consequently, the means of changing it cannot be specified in advance, but must be worked out in the actual situation.

Socialism is not a monolithic structure; the precise form that it should take in South Africa can only be determined in South Africa; and that only by those in whose interest it is that the present system be changed, which means primarily, almost exclusively, by Blacks. Whites have no more proprietary rights over socialism than they do over Christianity; and since the understanding and practice of both are historically and socially conditioned, they must both be reinterpreted in and by South African conditions. This follows from the nature of socialism; not simply from some romantic idea about Africans being naturally socialist.

The values of primitive communalism may still be valid, but they can no longer be expressed in that form. 'Primitive communalism,' as Nyerere says, 'is (equally) doomed. The moment the first enamel pot, or factory woven cloth is imported into a self-sufficient communal society, the economic and social structure of that society receives its deathblow. Afterwards it is merely a question of time, and of whether the members of that community will be participants or victims in the new economic order.' (*loc.cit.*, p. 441). Blacks have undoubtedly been, and still are, the victims of the present economic system; how they become participants is a new one is primarily their problem. But socialism provides the only alternative; and it is only from a socialist standpoint that Whites can welcome and encourage Black initiative in determining the form of the new order.

Some dogmatic socialists tend to scoff at the idea of a particularly African form of socialism. Such a view might be understandable on the part of those who want to manipulate the new order, but it does not seem to be a very scientific one. Socialism has in fact taken different forms in different places - 'Anyone who though that socialism would be the same in Cuba as it is in Bulgaria is a fool or a C.I.A. agent.' (H. Aptheker, in *From Hope to Liberation,* eds. N. Piediscalzi and R.G. Thobaben, p. 55) - and there is every reason that it should. Socialism 'is born of history and geography; it was born in the nineteenth century in Western Europe. Conceived in that milieu, it was essentially designed to analyze and transform it. Marx often affirmed this. The proof is that today, in these same countries, scientists and philosophers, writers, and artists, while assimilating Marx's methodological contributions, have gone beyond, shaded and enriched them to penetrate realities no longer of the nineteenth but of the twentieth century' (Senghor, *On African Socialism,* p. 77). If socialism is to penetrate and transform the realities of present-day South Africa, it must be re-conceived by those who understand and experience those realities, and there are increasing signs of Black political groups doing this.

It is true that attempts at implementing 'African socialism' in other

African States have not been notably successful. But this is not due entirely to personal abuses and/or the lack of socialist 'theory'. The condition in which these countries were left at the time of independence also plays a large part. Most, if not all, of them achieved political independence but not cultural and economic independence. They have remained dependent both on the former 'mother country' and on international capitalism which continues to exploit them under the guise of 'development'. So-called 'aid', which is in fact restitution, from First World countries increases this dependence. There are, of course, other factors too, including time. Nyerere has said that after ten years Tanzania is still only on the path towards socialism and it will be more than another thirty years before socialism is established (*Daily News*, 24 Feb. 1977).

Being a socialist in South Africa does not mean looking to Russia rather than to American for liberation, it means looking to South Africa. Obviously, outside forces will play a part, probably a decisive one, in bringing about change, but the imposition of any preconceived system cannot lead to the true liberation of South Africans, Black or White. There is in fact more danger of America seeking to impose its idea of liberation than there is of any socialist power doing so. In many respects it would be better for South Africa to remain in its present semi-colonialised state than to be 'coca-cola-nised'. If the Carter administration is sincerely concerned about human rights, there are many things it could and should do before setting itself up as the moral guardian of Southern Africa and indeed the whole world. It could, for instance, stop Americans consuming half the world's resources; it could stop possessing enough nuclear armaments to annihilate everybody several times over; it could stop polluting literally the whole world: 'When scientists discovered lead and mercury from American gasolene and industry in both polar regions, they discovered the totality of America's physical presence in the human family: pollutants whose effect is irreversable brain damage, transmitted from American producers and consumers to "the living air" and ultimately to "the mind of man".' (J. Illo, *New Blackfriars*, July 1973).

If America goes on its way unchecked there will not be any humans left to have rights: 'American pollutants, whether economic or military, are especially potent in transforming man, in effecting a decline in his ability to be a man. The radiation from American nuclear explosions, like the lead from American gasolene and the mercury from American factories, produces a decay of the human brain and of the human capacity for thought and moral decision.' (Illo, *loc.cit.*). There are doubtless many very good Americans, and Jimmy Carter may even be one of them, but their whole system is very sick: ask the Blacks or the Berrigans; the Cubans or the Vietnamese. The world cannot afford, physically or morally, an extension of America in Africa. America might, however, learn something from Africa: 'perhaps one day, if the human race survives long enough, the Americans will absorb something of the general culture of older peoples, will rejoin, in a sense, the human race' (A. Black, *New Blackfriars,* Dec. 1976, p. 541).

The tendency of White South Africans to ape the American way of life is simply contemptible, but it is sad to see Black leaders apparently pinning their hopes for change on American intervention. On the day that I wrote the above paragraphs two reports appeared on the same page in a newspaper; the one was datelined New York and the other Tokyo. In the one Bishop Tutu was quoted as saying, 'We still believe even at this late hour that human suffering, bloodshed and hatred can be turned into peace with direct American involvement and identification with the oppressed. America does have the necessary *peaceful weapons* to assist in the restoration of the *dignity of man* in Southern Africa.' The other read: 'Kidneys from aborted foetuses, shipped *"live"* from South Korea to the United States, may only be a small part of the world-wide traffic in human organs which are used by the US army for *biological warfare* research, it is alleged here.' (*Daily News,* 14 March 1977; my italics). It was admitted in Washington that some of the 'foetal material' did go to the army hospital. Such respect for human dignity Africa can surely do without.

This does not mean that I would prefer Russian domination to American. I do not believe that Russia has the same interest in dominating South Africa that America has. Even if Russia does have imperialist tendencies, it does not pursue them with the religious fervour of the moral crusader, as America does. In any event, the best safeguard against the imposition of Soviet socialism, to which I would object on both Christian and socialist grounds, is the development of an indigenous form of socialism. Imperialism, whether military, monetary, cultural or intellectual, is a contradiction of socialism.

The political choice facing a Christian, in South Africa as elsewhere in the world today, is between capitalism and socialism. The question of the racial discriminatory or multiracial nature of society can only arise within the framework of a capitalist system, which of its nature demands inequality and exploitation. In a genuinely socialist system the question of racial discrimination would not arise. Since there would be no need to exploit anybody, there would be no need to discriminate against anybody. As an historical legacy, there might be a certain amount of racial *prejudice* to be overcome, but that is not a *political* problem. The political problem is racial discrimination. Once the conflict of interests, which is the root cause of such discrimination, has been resolved, the practice, together with all forms of exploitation, would cease; at the same time the main breeding ground of racial prejudice would be disposed of.

chapter 9
The Present Role of Socialism

Socialism does not provide a solution for the problems of South Africa. There *is* no solution to these problems; certainly not in the sense that somewhere, in someone's mind or in some book, in a CIA or KGB file, there is a blueprint, which, given a bit of goodwill on all sides, could be implemented in South Africa. A solution cannot be *found;* it can only be worked out. And socialism provides the framework for doing that. The element of flexibility in the socialist approach is one of its chief advantages. Others, particularly Christians perhaps, arrogantly assume that they have all the answers and spend all their time trying to persuade everybody to accept them. Socialism does not claim to have ready-made answers; but it does have the means both of understanding the problems and of working towards a solution.

The dominant feature of the present South African political scene is undoubtedly the growth of Black Consciousness. More and more 'progressive' Whites are coming to recognise the power and positive content of this Movement. Some, therefore, see the role of Whites as being simply to be, in the words of the Roman Catholic Bishops, 'on the side of Black Consciousness'. Some socialists, on the other hand, are chary of this Movement, because they consider that it detracts from an understanding of the root cause of oppression. I believe, however, that both approaches are wrong. Firstly, because Black Consciousness is not a political *system;* it is a politicising *movement,* which, on the basis of its own definition of its aims, can only be systematised within a socialist system. Secondly, and obviously, Black Consciousness is for Blacks and I do not know that they are particularly concerned whether or not Whites are 'on its side'; the question for Whites is how to respond to it; and this can only be answered from a socialist standpoint. Thirdly, both the Black youth and the official Black Consciousness organisations,* the Black People's Convention (BPC) and the South African Students

Organisation (SASO), have shown and stated that they reject far more than the external signs of racial discrimination. Black Consciousness, therefore, is not a substitute for socialism, nor is it a threat to socialism; socialism and Black Consciousness are complementary.

SASO, within which Black Consciousness originated, has stated that 'the basic tenet of Black Consciousness is that the Black man must reject all value systems that seek to make him a foreigner in the country of his birth and reduce his basic human dignity. The Black man must build up his own value system, see himself as self-defined and not as defined by others'. Black Consciousness, therefore, cannot lead to a capitalist system, because capitalism is, of its very nature, a 'foreign' system with its own preconceived values and definition of man as an essentially private individual who is motivated by the desire for personal gain. The incompatibility of Black Consciousness and capitalism is confirmed by the practice of the proponents of Black Consciousness who do not accept Black capitalists as Black but see them as 'non-Whites'. Socialism, however, because of its essentially historical character, cannot be described as a 'foreign' system; its methodology is geographically foreign in origin, but as a value system it is not closed and predetermined as capitalism is. A Black man, like any other man, can only be free to define himself - which necessarily entails defining his relationships with others - in a socialist society where he is freed from the constraints placed upon him by his place in the production process.

The rejection of capitalism which is necessarily implied in SASO's definition of Black Consciousness also explains why Whites can only respond from a socialist standpoint. Black Consciousness demands *a complete* rejection of the present system; so does socialism. Capitalism, however 'enlightened', does not. It is concerned only with adapting the system to suit its own purposes. Despite what they may *say* therefore, it is not possible for Whites to be *in fact* 'on the side of Black Consciousness', if they are capitalists. To be a capitalist, whether one is White or Black, it is necessary to be part of the present system; it is not possible to be part of that system and at the same time support its complete rejection. Further, Black Consciousness, by exploding the myths which serve as a rationalisation for racial discrimination, does lead to an understanding of the true nature of Black oppression. Even if it did not, I think that it would be an essential prerequisite for such an understanding.

More recently, however, the Black Consciousness Movement's rejection of capitalism has been made more explicit. There is no need for a socialist to feel threatened because this is not expressed in 'classical' socialist terms. South Africa is not a 'classical' capitalist society and there is no 'classical' way in which it can be changed. What exactly SASO

and BPC mean by 'African Communalism' is not yet clear, but it
certainly involves a rejection of capitalism. They have in common with
socialism a clear realisation that no meaningful change can be brought
about by collaboration with capitalists, be they Americans or Progressive
Reform South Africans. The Soweto youth by their reaction to the
Kissinger visit, for example, showed that they were quite aware of the
wider dimensions of the problem.

Black Consciousness has, to a large extent, already fulfilled its primary
purpose, of making Blacks aware of their identity and dignity. It remains,
however, the major force for change. Any attempted 'solution' which
ignores it can only aim either at a compromise with capitalism and the
consequent betrayal of the interests of the majority of Blacks or at the
imposition of a 'foreign' system.

Both Christians and socialists acknowledge that the main impetus for
change must, and can only, come from Blacks. They bear the brunt of
the oppression and if they are not prepared to change it there is nothing
anybody else can do. However, this does not mean on the one hand, that
all Blacks are oracles; nor, on the other, that Whites have no contribution
to make.

Christians have a particular obligation to listen to Blacks, since as
Jurgen Moltmann says, 'On the basis of faith in the crucified there is,
from the Christian viewpoint, a sort of "messianism of the poor". For in
God's future the poor will save the rich (*Luke* 16) and not the rich the
poor. The manifesto of the Christian theology of hope consists of the
beatitudes of Jesus which proclaim the future of God's kingdom to the
poor, the mourners, and the hungry.' (*In Search of a Theology of
Development,* Sodepax Report, p. 99). In South Africa, however, there
are conflicting voices which claim to speak on behalf of the poor; it is
therefore necessary to have a norm for deciding what is the true source
of the 'messianism of the poor'. In making this decision a White man is
not interfering in a Blacks-only squabble; he is fulfilling his own
obligation and determining his own response. (Somewhat ironically, it is
Blacks who claim to favour a multiracial strategy leading to a multiracial
society who are the first to deny a White man the right to do this - unless
he is a capitalist.) This decision cannot be based on racial considerations;
it must be based on concern for the poor. Such concern cannot be
expressed in a capitalist system, since capitalism does not and cannot
serve the interests of the poor. The present system is essentially
capitalist and so is the only White alternative. Any Black, therefore, who
collaborates or compromises with either of these cannot claim to be the
'messiah' of the poor. Capitalism does not become less evil and less
morally repugnant to a Christian simply because it has the blessing of a
Black; that would be extreme racism.

The appeals of 'homeland' leaders, for example, to foreign investors were certainly not very 'messianic' in tone. Chief Wessels Mota of Basuto Qwa Qwa advised them to 'Stop pussyfooting around. If you want a nice, fat, highly-profitable overseas operation invest in SA. But make sure you build your factory in a Black area.' (Labour is even cheaper and more exploitable there than elsewhere in South Africa.) Chief Gatsha Buthelezi assured them that KwaZulu could offer 'problem-free labour resources'; free no doubt from problems like strikes and demands for higher wages. (Quoted in *Financial Mail,* 11 Oct. 1974). The colour of the people making such statements has nothing to do with their value. The destiny of Whites, both religiously and politically, is bound up with that of Blacks. Whites, therefore, have the right and duty to oppose the words or actions of anyone, Black or White, who would lead them to share the common fate of living under a capitalist system. The only Black voice that Whites can and must listen to is that which genuinely serves the interests of the poor by rejecting capitalism.

The relevancy of anybody's, Black or White, contribution to change primarily depends on his/her relationship to the present system. But while some Blacks can, and do, *become* part of the system, all Whites *are,* in varying degrees, part of the system and are identified as such by their colour. We all contribute to the capitalist nature of our society; and that on the side of the exploiters. We are all probably infected with some elements of racism. (Do you *never* make a generalisation about Blacks? When told that some people have been looking for you, do you ask whether they were Black or White? True, some might ask in order to estimate the chances of their being security police.) We cannot even begin to make a contribution towards change until we have freed ourselves, as far as is possible, from participation in and contamination by the present system. We therefore need consciously to challenge and to reject both the capitalist values and the racist rationalisations on which the system is based. Socialism poses this challenge. Whites who respond to this challenge can at least contribute to the rejection of the present system which is the essential prerequisite for radical change.

The rejection of capitalist values, which is a Christian duty as well as a socialist objective, is not simply a matter of changing one's intellectual convictions. The claim to be a socialist, like the claim to be a Christian, is not true unless it is expressed in practice. While on the one hand, it is not possible to start building a socialist system piecemeal fashion within a capitalist system, there is no point, on the other, in professing to be a socialist while living in a mansion and dining off silver plate while Black servants hover discreetly in the background overhearing snatches of conversation about the distribution of wealth. (There are such 'socialists' in South Africa.) On a personal level it is difficult to distinguish between socialist values and Christian virtues; the purpose of socialism is to create the social and political structures which facilitate the practice of these values or virtues. But their practice on a personal level is necessary for both socialists and Christians if their professed beliefs are to have any credibility.

There is a tendency, which I have followed myself, of referring to the rejection of 'White' values, but there is obviously nothing inherently objectionable about the quality of 'whiteness'; this is simply shorthand for 'whitewashed', Western, capitalist values. Western civilisation doubtless has much to offer any society (Mozart and cricket spring immediately to mind); it is its apparently indissoluble marriage to capitalism, with its individualism, greed, exploitation and waste of people and natural resources, that is the cause of its present decadent state. It is quite literally in a state of decay, because apart from any moral considerations, the world's physical resources cannot continue to meet the demands of the present rate of consumption of the minority of 'haves'. If you are eating a piece of prime beef, the production of which entailed the consumption of enough grain to feed half a dozen starving people, the fact that you listen with appreciation to Mozart while doing so does not make you any more civilised, or any less guilty.

Capitalism in South Africa has dehumanised both Blacks and Whites. Any contribution, therefore, which Whites might be able to make on a cultural, technological, or any other level, will only be of any significance when both have rediscovered their humanity and are living in, or at least working positively towards, a society where this humanity is truly recognised. There is little of positive value that Whites can do in the meantime; nothing if they remain dedicated to capitalism.

It would be neither possible nor desirable for everybody in South Africa to live in the manner that some Whites do. The richness of the few is as obscene as the poverty of the many; because the former is the cause of the latter. Socialism does not idealise poverty or asceticism; it appreciates that for a man to be fully human his material needs must be met. It also appreciates, however, that *human* fulfilment cannot be found in the enjoyment of material things *at the expense of other people;* it might be pleasurable, but it is not human. No man, for example, *needs* half a dozen or more houses for his personal use; and he can only have them, as some White South Africans do, because there are millions of people who are herded together in compounds, or dumped in resettlement villages or inadequately housed in 'townships'. One mining magnate occupies more living space than several hundred of his employees put together. The condition of the employees in the compounds is obviously an inhuman one. But so is that of the mining magnate; because you cannot have one without the other. It is not simply the luxury in which the rich live that socialists object to, but the price that has to be paid for it. Because of the price that has to be paid, such luxury dehumanises both the rich and the poor. Although there are only a few ultra-rich, like the mining magnates, as long as they are held up as exemplars, as they are in a capitalist system, we cannot have a human society.

The unquestioning acceptance of capitalist values has made Christians, as well as others, blind to the dehumanising effects of the capitalist system, on capitalist and worker alike. Socialism performs a service to humanity in general and to Christianity in particular by creating an awareness of this.

It would be anachronistic to judge opposition movements of another historical period in the light of our present understanding and to expect them to have seen their role in socialist terms. Blacks have, of course, opposed White domination ever since the White man came to South Africa. At first this was expressed in military conflict. In the early days of its political expression it continued to be motivated almost exclusively by nationalist interests. Later there tended to be an assumption that two 'revolutions' were needed: a national one and a social one. It was assumed that racial discrimination had to be overcome first and then attention could be given to the building of a just economic order. The failure of such an approach, or rather the suppression of such opposition, cannot simply be ascribed to faulty strategy; it might well have been the best strategy for that time. There is no guarantee that another approach would have succeeded then, nor that it will succeed in the immediate future; there is also the power of the forces ranged against it to be considered. Only one thing is certain: without the long and heroic struggle that has already taken place, the prospects for the creation of a just society would be infinitely dimmer than they are at the moment.

It is now apparent, however, that racial discrimination cannot be overcome independently of the elimination of economic exploitation; it can only be given a different name, and made more 'acceptable' - in capitalist terms.

It is now in the interest of the 'enlightened capitalists', and even of the Nationalists, that racial discrimination be seen as a surface wound on the South African body politic which can be treated without upsetting the basic metabolism of that body. But, although the wound is clearly evident on the surface, it was not inflicted from outside; it is the symptom of a more serious, internal disorder. If people continue to accept the capitalist diagnosis, they will seek to apply the capitalist 'remedy' and will never cure the cause of the disorder. Church leaders, particularly, concerned as they may be about applying a remedy, seem quite incapable of questioning the validity of this diagnosis. The liberal capitalist presuppositions of the Roman Catholic Bishops, for example, are evident in every one of their twenty-one points of what the Catholic newspaper described as a 'Programme for Social Justice' (*Southern Cross,* 27 Feb. 1977).

This 'Programme' is certainly an improvement on anything previously produced by Church leaders of any denomination; it does not confine itself to vague general statements, but tries to be specific. However, the document should rather be called 'A guide on how to live with your conscience in an unjust society'. It does note in one point that 'evangelisation includes transforming the concrete political structures that oppress people' but none of the other points says anything about changing such structures. It is *assumed* that all that is wrong with the structures of both Church and society is the extent to which racism is practised within them. The Bishops thus propose 'to signify, by the appointment of black priests to the charge of white parishes, the breaking away by the Church from the prevailing social and political system'. Such an action is not particularly significant, and it certainly does not involve breaking away from the present *political* system. There would be no need for the Nationalists to object to a Black priest ministering to Whites, provided he adhered to *their* definition of 'religion' and *their* definition of 'politics'. The rejection of these definitions, in *practice,* would involve a breakaway from the prevailing system. The preaching of an individualistic, spiritualised idealist 'Christianity', no matter what the colour of the preacher and his congregation, does not challenge *any* political system. The appointment of a Black priest to a White parish might be useful for the education of Whites; it might help them to overcome some of their racial prejudice. As such it might be worthwhile, but it is not a political action. The political problem is eliminating the cause of racial discrimination; racial prejudice has little to do with that cause.

One's hopes are raised when one reads that the Bishops propose 'to devote serious study to the re-evaluation of the meaning and use of money'. This surely must lead to an examination of the root cause of the problems of exploitation and social relationships. Such hopes, however, are soon dashed when one finds that this only refers to 'how much it (money) should be seen as belonging to the local parish and how much to the church collectively'. Can this really be called a 'serious study'? Does not money also have something to do with capitalism and consequently with the whole ordering of our society? Where does the money, which they intend allocating on the 'principle of communalising church funds', come from? Christianity is concerned with far more than the question of distribution of wealth; it is also concerned about the nature of wealth, how it is produced and its function in the life of the individual and of society. Such questions can only be tackled within the framework of socialism.

The Bishops acknowledge the need for promoting an 'awareness of injustice and social problems as essential to evangelisation', but there is no sign of they themselves being aware of them. The only awareness that they can, and do, promote is a capitalist one, but they cannot maintain that this is 'essential to evangelisation'. The proposals contained in this 'Programme' could be fully implemented and the Nationalists would not be threatened, Whites would not be challenged and Blacks would continue to be exploited; perhaps a little less than they are now, if they happened to be employed by the Roman Catholic Church. The Bishops admit that the Catholic Church is 'lagging behind in witness to the Gospel in matters of social justice'. But it will lag even further behind if it adjusts its pace to that of its more reactionary members. If it is still necessary 'to strive for the elimination of terms . . . which . . . are derogatory and even insulting and to eradicate all differentiation on purely racial grounds in the treatment of persons at presbyteries, convents and church institutions', there is no chance of the Church playing a meaningful part in bringing about radical change. Events in South Africa will not wait for such people. It is axiomatic that such practices are abhorrent to Christians; a 'Programme for Social Justice' must start many steps ahead of that. To start such a 'Programme' at the level of telling people not to call African men 'native boys', is like starting a course in spiritual direction for nuns by warning them to avoid bestiality and incest.

In addition to the capitalist presuppositions, the Westernness of the Bishops' approach is also shown by their 'idealist' understanding of both Christianity and politics. They acknowledge, for example, the importance of consulting with lay people, priests and religious, particularly Blacks, so that they may 'participate with the bishops in arriving at policy on church life and apostolate, but not on doctrinal and canonical matters'. But it is not possible to separate 'policy' and 'doctrine' in this way and still to arrive at any meaningful and realistic conclusions; the two are necessarily inter-related. Further, even in the most traditional theologies, the *'sensus fidelium'* - the opinion of the people - is a recognised vehicle of the teaching authority of the Church. It is particularly important, in a situation which the official custodians of doctrine do not experience and consequently do not really understand, that the doctrine be reinterpreted in the light of the practice, or 'policy' of those who do.

I am not being hypercritical, not attaching particular blame to the Catholic Bishops; they are obviously more concerned about social evils than are most Whites. Their statement, however, provides a good illustration of how the lack of a conscious political perspective and of a specifically socialist analysis nullifies the goodwill and concern of many Christians and non-Christians alike. If Bishops are going to talk about political and social matters, as indeed they should, what they say must make sense on social and political terms; if it does not make sense in those terms, it does not make sense in theological terms. This particular document, like so many statements by Christian bodies, has little, if any, political relevance, because it is not politically grounded - except in so far as it *assumes* the validity and immutability of liberal capitalism. The 'unemployed, industrial workers in general and migrant workers in particular . . . political prisoners, detainees, (and) banned people', for example, do not need 'the creation of communities among them by specially appointed priests, religious and lay workers'. The first three groups need to organise *themselves* into trade unions, and the latter three need people to carry on the work that they were doing.

It is not possible to break away 'from the prevailing social and political system' in a specifically Christian way. The system is an essentially capitalist one and can only be broken away from in a socialist way, which is, therefore, the way for Christians. The *assumption* of a capitalist viewpoint is no less political than an explicit commitment to socialism; but it leads to an un-Christian and ineffective approach to social and political problems.

This lack of a conscious political perspective and the implicit acceptance of a capitalist one bedevils any attempt by Christians to judge both the morality and the political implications of specific issues. Thus, for example, church people, both in South Africa and overseas, spend a great deal of time discussing the question of foreign investment in South Africa. All the arguments in favour of so-called 'constructive engagement', and even some of those used against it, are, however, quite irrelevant; because they are based on a false analysis of the actual situation. Since it is not simply the racial character of the system that is immoral, but the system itself, there is no point in seeking either to prove or disprove that investment can change this racial character. It obviously cannot change the system, because it is, by definition, an investment *in* the system. The question of morality only arises if either the role of capitalism is ignored or capitalism is accepted as an ideal. But the former is politically, and therefore also morally, irresponsible, and the latter is demonstrably un-Christian.

The system itself is immoral because of its capitalist nature, therefore any participation in it has the same immoral character; no number of beneficial side effects can change this. The Nationalists seem to be much more aware of the support given to their system by foreign investment than their opponents are. Otherwise, why would they go to great lengths to encourage it and why would they 'discourage' people from advocating the withdrawal of foreign investment by charging them under the Terrorism Act? If one is prepared to be purely pragmatic, materialistic (in the capitalist sense), politically naive, and un-Christian, one could try to make out a case for 'constructive engagement', but it could not be called a 'moral' argument. The question of the morality of foreign investment, as well as of its political and economic efficacy can only be answered in either a capitalist or socialist way. If one is a capitalist one will be in favour of it, and therefore against radical change; a socialist will oppose it in favour of radical change. There is no need for all the intellectual gymnastics, costly research, and spurious moral arguments, about the *effects* of investment *in South Africa.* The only effect it can have is the development of capitalism, which is the cause of the present problems and, if the 'enlightened capitalists' have their way, will be the cause of future problems.

The same sort of argument applies to numerous other issues, such as boycotts, sporting ties, trade links, diplomatic relations, integrated schools, 'development' projects, etc. One cannot base one's political or moral stance in regard to such matters on the real or imagined influence they have on the degree of racial prejudice of White South Africans. To do so is to presuppose the validity of the capitalist analysis and 'solution'. The question, both morally and politically, is whether or not they support the present system; if they do they thereby entrench discrimination. A conscious and critical understanding of the true nature of the politico-economic system is, therefore, an essential part of any moral judgement about specific actions which relate to that system. There is no distinct Christian understanding; nor is there a separate social and political morality. It is the Churches' *assumption* of capitalist norms that is responsible for them, in general, supporting foreign investment, trade, diplomatic and other relationships, and opposing boycotts.

It is not my purpose here to expound upon the benefits which would derive to all from the actual establishment of a socialist system. I am only concerned with the essential function that a socialist analysis and perspective can perform in the present situation. It is only from a socialist standpoint that Whites can relate and respond to Black political initiative; that we can benefit from the 'messianism of the poor'. Only socialism effectively challenges the values - individualism, wealth, etc. - on which the present system is based and which are the accepted values of virtually all Whites. The acceptance of such values perpetuates a system which is the antithesis of Christianity or at most seeks to replace it with one that is equally repugnant; whereas socialism provides an 'historically scientific way of making love efficacious' (Bonino, *Christians and Marxists,* p. 115). Anybody, therefore, who claims to be concerned about loving his neighbour, and not simply about thinking that he should, is morally obliged at least to examine the claims of socialism and to reappraise his understanding and practice of Christianity in the light of its criticisms. That we should love our neighbour is a Christian duty; how we can do this effectively and practically in a particular historical time and place is a political problem, which only socialism can solve. Capitalism does not even try; it is concerned with things, not people.

We, as Whites, therefore, do not have simply to sit and twiddle our thumbs while waiting for Blacks to 'get their thing together' and change the system. We are not 'the oppressed' but we are in a sense oppressed, and liberation can no more be *imposed* on us than it can on Blacks. Blacks can help to liberate us, but they have nothing to offer us in terms of capitalist values. As Christians, we believe that the ultimate source of all liberation is Jesus Christ. But we cannot hear what he says or do what he would have us do if we are more concerned about trying to be rich than about trying to be human; we cannot do both. The only programme of action for Whites is: stop trying to get rich and start trying to be human. Much of the effort that Whites put into doing things for Blacks is a distraction from this essential task and serves only to further the dehumanisation of both Blacks and Whites. It is not part of our Christian duty to make Blacks capitalists. Nor am I suggesting that we should try to *make* them socialists; you cannot make people socialist any more than you can make them Christians. Both Christianity and socialism are *offered;* and that primarily by example. As Christians, we are on the side of the poor, but the only political system that furthers the interests of the poor is socialism.

For Whites, therefore, socialism is a duty, for Blacks it is the natural, logical demand of their condition as poor and oppressed. Socialism helps to liberate both Whites and Blacks: Whites from the evils of having too much; Blacks from the evils of having too little.

chapter 10
'What Can We Do?'

Many, genuinely concerned, Christians in South Africa are desperately asking: What can we *do? Assuming the present White understanding of both Christianity and politics,* the only answer to that question is: 'Nothing.' I suspected this before I began writing this book; I am now utterly convinced of it. Any action which is based on such an understanding can only be at best conscience-salving; at worst, counter-productive.

Preoccupation with racism, even for the purpose of overcoming it, leads to practices which are themselves racist. Thus, for example, the general injunctions made by Church leaders to their White congregants to become involved in community development projects for Blacks, discussion groups with Blacks, teaching Blacks, implies an assumption, which can only be described as racist, that all Whites always have something to offer, simply because they are White. But just because a person is White it does not follow that he/she knows anything about community development; in fact the chances are that because of his/her Western, individualistic outlook, he/she would not even begin to understand the community aspect. Even for Whites to share the skills they do have is not necessarily a good thing, if the cost of such sharing is an increased dependence of Blacks on Whites. The ability to sew, for example, is not essential to a person's human dignity, but self-respect is. If the teaching of skills elicits the same sort of response from Blacks as that published in the newsletter of a Roman Catholic parish - 'We would like to thank the White madams who taught us to sew, cook, etc. We poor Blacks were in darkness and they are bringing us to the light' - Blacks would be better off, as human beings, without the skills.

Without doubting the sincerity and goodwill of many Whites, I do not believe that the vast majority are presently *capable* of radically changing South African society. They do not know what radical change means, because they do not know what the root cause of the present problem is, and they do not see the need for it; all they see the need for is 'allowing' Blacks to become part of a White system. As long as material self-interest, as defined in capitalist terms, is the predominant aim of

Whites, they have every reason to oppose radical change. If Christians seek to give a veneer of respectability to this aim, as they have done and are still doing, they are part of the opposition to change. A 'Christianity' that has been formed, or rather, deformed, by and in South African society cannot respond to the 'messianism of the poor'.

The Nationalists claim that apartheid is necessary to defend Western, Christian civilisation, and the basis of much 'Christian' opposition is the rejection of this claim. But, like John Davies, I have come to 'realize that there is truth in the claim - that apartheid is a development of certain western assumptions concerning human identity, concerning authority, freedom, wealth and success, and that the Christian tradition has been captured and distorted to lend support to these assumptions' (*Good News in Galatians*, p. 8).

John Davies' comment is an apt summary of what this book is about. We have examined some of the presuppositions which have led to a distortion of Christianity and have made it impossible for White Christians wholeheartedly and effectively to oppose the present system. They cannot oppose it wholeheartedly because they share the same capitalist values; they cannot oppose it effectively because an 'idealist' understanding of Christianity divorces religion from reality and confines it to a private, intellectual, 'spiritual' sphere where it remains untouched by political or social influences.

To liberate ourselves from enslavement to a Western and capitalist understanding of man and society, and hence of Christianity, and to be able to contribute towards the process of change, a revolution in our way of understanding, and consequently practising, both Christianity and politics is required. I do not claim to have expressed this understanding, nor even to have it and act according to it myself. Such an understanding cannot be arrived at in isolation, nor simply by intellectual study and discussion. We cannot be *given* an understanding, nor can we be issued with a set of directives. All we can be given is a *method* for arriving at an understanding and practice and for seeing the relationship between the two; a method for arriving at a praxis.

'Liberation Theology' provides a way of doing theology; socialism provides a way of doing politics. But since 'doing theology' necessarily entails political action and since there can be no purely theological or Christian answer to political questions, the two 'ways' must be integrated. The 'doing', however, can only be done; it cannot be taught or thought.

'Doing theology' is like crossing a river, not by a bridge or even an established arrangement of stepping stones, but by a haphazardly placed collection of rocks. You can see where you want to go but you cannot sit down and plan exactly which rocks you will use to get there. The only way to reach the goal is to test each rock as you go. You must first put your foot on the rock before you can decide whether you think it is safe. But you will only *know* that it is safe once you have stood on it. No map can be provided for such a crossing because some once firm rocks become loose while others become firmly lodged in the river-bed.

Traditional theologians assume, firstly, that they have a map, and secondly, that the crossing can only be made from where they are standing. But, as we have seen, neither theology nor the Bible can provide us with a map. And the fact that we have not yet even begun to make the crossing should make us at least question whether our proposed starting point is the best one. There are in fact many crossing points; though they all entail taking risks. The oppressed have the motivation to take these risks, so they are the ones most likely to find the way.

The agenda for change in South Africa is being drawn up by Blacks and will largely be carried out by them. This, I believe, both as a Christian and as a socialist, is not only the way it should be, but is the only way it can be, and is the way it will be, despite the blandishments of *any* Superpower. This is not because of any virtue inherent in Blackness, but because they are the oppressed. Blacks, however, can only liberate themselves from the evil of having too little by at the same time liberating Whites from the evil of having too much. Whites, therefore, are part of the same struggle, though in a different way. We cannot decide to leave the actual struggle to Blacks while we busy ourselves with planning the future society; the shape of the future society will be determined by the nature and outcome of the struggle.

I do not have such faith in democracy that I believe the majority is always and necessarily right and that therefore everything that Blacks do is right. I am not concerned with either their numbers or their colour, but with their condition as oppressed and the rights and power that this gives them. The rejection of oppression is necessary for both the oppressed and the oppressor, but only the oppressed can do it. Belief in the ability of the oppressed to throw off opposition is not, for the Christian, based on a blind faith in the Black man, but on faith that where evil is being overcome the Spirit is at work.

Blacks have made it clear that the first item on the agenda is the complete rejection of the present system. I suspect that some Whites do not really believe that the situation is as bad as Blacks say it is. But since they are the victims of the system we can only take their word (and actions) for it that the system affects them in such a way that they can only be liberated if it is completely changed.

Whites must agree, *in practice,* with this first item if we are to have any say about the rest of the agenda. We cannot identify with Blacks in their rejection; we can only identify by our own rejection. Our relationship to the system and the way we are affected·by it are different, therefore our rejection must be different. Even if it were possible for us physically to identify with Blacks, we could not impose on ourselves a history of oppression. Passionate protestations of identification with Blacks are meaningless expressions of romantic desires, if they are not a reflection of what one is actually doing in practice. A real, as opposed to a purely verbal, rejection must be based on an understanding of the real cause of oppression; otherwise we will continue to tilt at the windmills which the Nationalists erect for us.

We have seen that this cause is the White man's desire for wealth, which could, and can, only be fulfilled by Whites retaining control of political power and using it to discriminate against, and to exploit, Blacks. Only by rejecting this aim can the present system be replaced by one that is human and therefore acceptable to Christians. Blacks have not yet succeeded in completely rejecting the present system, so neither they nor we can expect Whites to have done so; but Blacks are obviously trying somewhat harder than Whites.

The question 'What can we do?' cannot be answered for us by others, even by Blacks. This conclusion does not arise from any desire to perpetuate a distinction between 'us' and 'them', but from a recognition of the fact that our situations, which both sociologically and theologically speaking influence our response, are different.

Both the staunchest supporters of Black Consciousness and their arch-enemies, 'White liberals', have stated that their ultimate aim is the creation of a multiracial society; they differ radically, however, about how this is to be achieved and about the form it should take. It is not possible to run a country simply by being multiracial; multiracialism is not a political system. It is not possible, therefore, to change the present political system simply by being concerned about the multiracial character of any activity. To respond to the racism of South African society by insisting on multiracialism at every available opportunity is to acknowledge the success of Nationalist propaganda.

Recognition of colour is not racism; preoccupation with it is. The liberal 'virtue' of colour blindness is in fact a paternalistic insult to Blacks; since, in effect, it means the acceptance of Blacks, despite the fact that they are Blacks, as Whites; whereas Blacks have said that they wish to affirm their Blackness. It is oppression and exploitation that we have to overcome, not cultural diversity; cultural differences do not divide people. We cannot, therefore, overcome the divisions of South African society by seeking to impose cultural uniformity. The advocating of 'colour blindness' is a response to, and gives credibility to, the Nationalists' claim that their policy is based on cultural diversity. Even if it were it would still be wrong, because man's common humanity is more important than any differences, however real they may be. But the Nationalists' policy is not, as they would like to have everybody believe that it is, based on cultural diversity; it is based on the 'need' to exploit, which follows from the White man's desire for wealth.

Racial discrimination cannot be overcome by multiracialism because it was not caused by racism; it can only be overcome in a society which is free from all exploitation. Whites can only contribute to the creation of such a society if we stop exploiting Blacks. The major contribution of Blacks is their refusal to be exploited. Blacks can, as they are doing, articulate this refusal and our response must be based on this; but this does not tell us exactly what we should do.

It is not possible for anyone to spell out in advance a detailed strategy for political change. But everybody who lives in society must, and in fact does, take a political stance. This is true also of the institutional churches. In the past, mainly by their silence, they have implicity taken a political stance on the side of the *status quo;* more recently they have tended to align themselves with a reformist or 'enlightened capitalist' approach to change, which is not concerned with, and is in any event incapable of, radically changing the present system. This is clearly not a valid response to the Black demand for a complete rejection of the system. There is much more that the Churches could do, without even breaking the law of the land.*

There are no laws which say, for example, that the Churches must run elitist schools and other institutions; or that they must own land and buildings; or that they must appoint priests or ministers as marriage officers, mayoral chaplains, or chaplains to the Defence Force. There is no reason for them not to stop these and similar practices immediately.

The Churches, between them all, must have assets worth hundreds of millions of rand. If these were all disposed of, the money could be made available to Blacks for them to do their own community development; there might even be sufficient for the establishment of a much-needed 'Strike Fund'. The fact that even hundreds of millions of rand would not change the situation and that it would soon be used up is irrelevant. Because the Churches would not be doing this for Blacks but *for themselves.* The ownership of these assets necessarily links the Churches with the present system; as do the other practices mentioned. If the Churches were to respond to the Blacks' rejection of the system by

---

*   While it is true that we, the members, are the Church, because of the present structures of the churches it is legitimate to distinguish between the role of the churches as institutions and the role of their members; as institutions they are, whether they should be or not, part of the power structures of society and they have decision-making bodies, which act independently of the individual members.

themselves rejecting these links, the Blacks would have performed a service for the Churches; any financial benefit to Blacks would be a side-effect.

The Churches only need their investments, land, buildings, etc., in order to maintain themselves in their present form. But the Churches, in their present form, are part of the problem. A rich Church can only function by being part of, or by compromising with, the existing social order. In South Africa the Churches themselves have condemned this order as unjust; it is therefore in their interests, as Churches, not to be tied to such a system. Churches should not own vast tracts of land in any society, but particularly not in a society where the main source of injustice is the fact that the vast majority of the population have been forcibly deprived of their land. In breaking off, as far as possible, their links with the present system, the Churches would not only be responding to Black demands, they would be being more true to their calling as Churches.

More importantly, from the point of view of the institutional Churches, there is no law, of God or man, that says that Whites must be the teachers of, and preachers to, Blacks. The word of God is addressed to the whole man in his particular historical and social situation; no one outside that situation can prescribe what the Christian response should be. This does not simply mean that only Blacks can make Christianity relevant to Blacks, but that only Blacks can tell anyone, White or Black, what the word of God means in their oppressive situation. What it means is also important to Whites for the understanding of our own response. It is not enough to consult with Blacks or to appoint a proportionate number of Blacks to Boards, Councils or hierarchies; in any event, it is probable that only those Blacks would be consulted or appointed who were so westernised that they would not be able to perform this function.

It is not a question primarily of the number of Blacks involved in the running of the Churches, but of the form that the Church itself should take in order to meet the needs of the oppressed. If the structures and organisation of the Churches remain White, there is no point in having people with Black faces running them. This does not mean that Blacks are necessarily better Christians than Whites, but that Blacks can more effectively correct the distortions that Whites have introduced into Christianity and can thus lead both Blacks and Whites to a more authentic practice of Christianity. A Black understanding is necessary because the Blacks are oppressed and because the present White understanding has been used as a legitimation of that oppression.

The Church must become the Church *of* the oppressed. The oppressed themselves must have the decisive say about what Christianity means in this situation. Consequently, they must determine the role and the structural forms of the Church.

It cannot be expected that any and every Black man can articulate the meaning of Christianity in an oppressive situation; that is the task of Black Theology. Black Theology addresses itself primarily to Blacks, but there is one clear and fundamental lesson that it can teach White Christians, namely, that any theology must start from and be concerned with the whole man; this is also the biblical view and the view of any theology of liberation. It is not, however, the view of most White Christians. Such a consideration might seem rather remote from a concern with a radical political commitment. But the assumption of a definition of man which divides him into material and spiritual, into body and soul, necessarily precludes a wholehearted commitment to the liberation of man. Liberation might be seen as important because the material part of man is important, but there are other more important things, because the spiritual part of man is more important. There can, therefore, be no real concern for *human* liberation; 'material' liberation is seen as being a precondition for, and subservient to, 'spiritual' liberation.

A theological response by Whites, specifically to Black Theology, does not lie in the development of a 'White Theology'. A White Theology would be the opposite of Black Theology, not a response to it. Black Theology is a theology of the oppressed; a White Theology would be a theology of the oppressors. Blacks are not oppressed *because* they are Black, but the oppressive system has succeeded in giving a 'negative value' to 'Black'; therefore, in order to overcome their oppression it is necessary for Blacks to affirm the positive values of being Black, which is what both Black Theology and Black Consciousness do. Whites are not oppressors *because* they are White, but the same oppressive system has given a 'positive value' to 'White'. Blacks, in defining themselves in Black terms instead of in White-imposed terms, are challenging the values of a system which judges 'Black' to be negative and 'White' to be positive. They do this by *affirming* their Blackness; but the White response cannot be to affirm their Whiteness; they must challenge the same values, though from a different perspective. Black Theology, therefore, performs a positive function, but a White Theology would not.

The present, distorted Christian practice is a product of what could be called a 'White Theology'. Its 'Whiteness', however, does not derive from the colour of the people who formulated it, but from the fact that they understood Christianity in a Western way and incorporated capitalist values into this understanding. A White response to Black Theology, therefore, consists of the formulation of a theology which will liberate Whites from the present meaning of White.

The fact that there is such a thing as Black Theology can help to make us aware of the need for this, but we have to decide how to do it. But to respond by being concerned about 'Whiteness' implies that there is something about the quality of Whiteness that makes people oppressors, which is obviously nonsense. The oppressive character of the present White understanding and practice of Christianity can only be overcome by a conscious substitution of a socialist perspective for the present assumption of a capitalist one. Only thus can the Churches begin to serve the interests of the oppressed and to challenge the present White value system.

If the institutional Churches were to sever their links with the present system and to take all possible steps to abandon their Whiteness, they would give credibility to their claim to be on the side of the oppressed. Further, it would no longer be necessary for them to ask, 'What can we do?' Ready-made answers would not be provided, but there would be so many specific situations which demanded a response that there would be no time to ask the question. At first there would doubtless be a very angry, if not hysterical, response from many Whites, threatening to leave, or actually leaving the Church, and taking their money with them. That would be a good start; it would provide a very good educational experience for both clergy and laity. This would not be a matter of abandoning Whites in favour of Blacks. Many people walked away, some of them sadly, when Christ stated his demands. The Churches would simply be stating these same demands for today, as 'revealed' by the 'messianism of the poor'.

In the past the Churches have softened these demands in order to retain their White membership; or perhaps more exactly, because Church leaders have shared the presuppositions and values of Whites in general, their approach has been congenial to Whites. In doing so, however, they have been more faithful to their Whiteness than they have been to God, albeit perhaps unwittingly, for 'every attempt to evade the struggle against alienation and the violence of the powerful and for a more just and a more human world is the greatest infidelity to God' (Gutierrez, op.cit., p. 272). It is possible that some Whites can only be led to question their understanding and practice of Christianity and the presuppositions on which these are based, by the institutional Churches actually taking radical steps to show that they are on the side of the oppressed instead of simply saying that they are.

Where such an approach would lead to, I do not know; but I have enough faith in God and in the oppressed to believe that it could only lead to a more authentic Christian practice than we have at present. It cannot, however, even be embarked upon if one assumes the sacrosanctness of the present structures of the Church and the definitiveness of the present understanding of Christianity. But these are products of a Western and capitalist orientated society; they have no claim to being Christian and their irrelevancy in the present South African context has been proved by experience.

The repercussions, however, would not be limited to internal Church structures: there would also be political implications. Any theology which, like Black Theology, is concerned with the whole man must lead to political action. Black Theology cannot give Whites a political programme; but it demands a political response from them.

There would also doubtless be 'legal' implications, since it is not necessary in South Africa actually to break any law in order to fall foul of the 'law'. Such a consideration, however, should not have any influence on a Christian response. Nor, on the other hand, is it necessary to look for martyrdom; that will be the necessary consequence of a Christian practice. The only real choice facing the Churches in that regard is who the executioner is going to be. If they continue with their present practice of trying to adapt the present system, there is little chance of any meaningful survival in a future South Africa. They will either be persecuted because of their co-operation with an evil system, or they will simply be ignored. If they wholeheartedly and radically oppose the present system, attempts will be made to destroy them; but that would be persecution for the cause of right, which is an occupational hazard for Christians.

It is not possible to listen and respond to the oppressed with a mental *tabula rasa*. We cannot understand the voice of the oppressed if what they say is interpreted within the categories of ancient Greek or medieval philosophy; we cannot respond if their needs are understood in capitalist terms. We can only respond on the basis of an historical understanding of Christianity, because that is the biblical understanding and the understanding on which Black Theology is based. An historical understanding of Christianity sees the political effectiveness of the Christian response as part of its Christianness. To be a Christian it is not enough to be concerned or morally outraged about the evils of society; one has the obligation of finding the most effective political means of eradicating them. We have seen that the only political system which points to the way of doing this in the South African situation is socialism. I do not expect Bishops or other Church leaders to preach socialism; I expect them to preach Christianity. But Christianity here and now means actually rejecting the present system.

The Church's primary task is to seek the Kingdom, not simply to preach it. Seeking the Kingdom demands political activity, which in turn requires political analysis and strategy. There is no neutral, specifically Christian analysis or strategy and socialism offers the only morally acceptable analysis and strategy. A socialist perspective is necessary, therefore, not only to enable Whites to respond politically to Black demands, but also to enable them to respond as Christians; or, rather, it does the latter *because* it does the former.

To serve the interests of the poor, instead of those of the rich, would be a real 'breakaway from the prevailing social and political system'. This breakaway cannot be made unless we understand what we are breaking away from, and the urgency for doing so. But it can be made without knowing where we are going to. This, as Ruben Alves points out, is what the Bible tells us to do. It does not give us any recipe or formula. 'The New Testament simply says: "Believe the good news" - somewhere, somehow it is happening. "Repent"; throw away your old stethoscope and find a way of hearing the heartbeat of the future already pulsating in a community. And "Be baptized": join it.' (*Tomorrow's Child,* p. 199).

Church leaders, however, are probably too attached to their old stethoscopes to be prepared to throw them away. The revolution in thinking and practice that is required for a real response to the demands of the oppressed would involve the destruction of the 'spiritual' and material edifices that they have built up (though they may not have much choice about the destruction of the material ones). Perhaps the most that can be hoped for is that they are capable of realising that they are not capable of taking the necessary steps. But they will only realise this if their ivory towers are stormed by militant Christians. Changing the Churches is a means of changing society, because they are part of society and share many of the same values.

Much of the exploitation in South African society has been, and still is, perpetrated in the name of 'Christianity'; and much 'Christian' preaching has undoubtedly contributed to people's passivity in the face of oppression. Christians, therefore, have an obligation to counteract this. The restructuring of the Churches and the development of new forms of worshipping, and other, communities, are also political actions. The form of the Church - its life-style, way of worship, etc. - must express the political concerns of its members; it is in this way that a Christian gives his explicitly Christian witness in the political sphere: by being part of a Church that shows in every aspect of its life that it has taken a firm political stance on the side of the oppressed.

In this way the Church fulfils its prophetic role; part of which consists in the public denunciation of the evils of society. But for this denunciation to be valid, it is not sufficient for Church leaders simply to denounce what *they* think is evil. A moral judgement on political matters cannot avoid being based on a particular political analysis. Church leaders in South Africa tend to *assume* the validity of a capitalist analysis; because of this, the Church not only faces the danger of which

Gutierrez warns the South American Church, it is already succumbing to it. This is the danger of allowing 'itself to be assimilated into a society which seeks certain reforms without a comprehensive critique. It is the danger of becoming functional to the system all over again, only this time to a system which tries to modernise and to suppress the most outrageous injustices without effecting any deep change' (*op.cit.*, p. 267). There is plenty, therefore, for Christians to do in combating the continued distortion of Christianity in the institutional Churches.

A Christian, however, also has the same political obligations in society as anybody else has, but there is no specifically Christian way of discharging these. There is no Christian way of going on strike, for example, but going on strike might well be the right thing for a Christian to do; whether it is or not is a political judgement, which is no more or less valid for Christians than for anybody else. There is no point, therefore, in Christians meeting together as Christians to discuss political problems, or forming their own separate organisations to work for political change. Many Christians seem to believe that political problems can be solved simply by expressing 'Christian concern' over them. But if a group of people, whether they are Christians or not, do not in fact understand the political and economic realities of the situation, they could discuss for ever and never come to a politically meaningful conclusion. This is like a group of people with no knowledge of geometry trying to explain the theorem of Pythagoras to each other. I am not suggesting that Christians have all the goodwill and moral motivation, while non-Christians have all the knowledge; but only that Christians do not have a monopoly of the truth and that Christians alone, as Christians, cannot fulfil their Christian obligation of being politically effective. There is a Christian motivation for, and meaning of, political involvement, but there is no Christian analysis, no Christian strategy, no Christian political option.

Christ has shown that he is concerned with the liberation of *people;* that this takes place is the important consideration, not who gets the credit titles. A Christian's place, therefore, is with those who are working for such liberation; and the first question he asks of them is how politically committed they are, not how 'holy' they are. In collaborating with others on the basis of a shared political commitment, one does not cease to be Christian, nor does one cease 'to be a witness of Jesus Christ or a "presence" of the Church - the Church in *diaspora* as it has been frequently said. His (a Christian's) faith, hope and love should find concrete reflection in his praxis. But this reflection will be (generally) totally incorporated in this praxis. Only faith discerns the presence of Jesus Christ!' (Bonino, *Doing Theology in a Revolutionary Situation*, p. 171).

Part of the reason for some Christians assuming that they, and they alone, can resolve complex political and social problems lies in their refusal to acknowledge the complexity of such problems. They assume that all political and social ills are caused by people's mental attitudes; all that is needed to change society, therefore, is the proposing of intellectual arguments and moral motivation for changing individuals. But social and political structures, which in so far as they are oppressive are the concrete manifestation of sin, are neither formed nor changed in that way. This is a matter of sociologically and historically verifiable fact, not a theological opinion. Theology must take account of this fact, if it is to be concerned with people and not with 'souls'.

The role of the Christian, or of any radically committed person, in relation to virtually all recognised White political or quasi-political organisations in South Africa, will be interpreted by such organisations as a negative one: stopping them continuing their present activities. But since these actions are counterproductive in terms of their relevancy to radical change, stopping them is a positive and necessary action. The present system has only lasted as long as it has because of the continual patching-up work done by well meaning, but uncritical, reformists. I am not suggesting that we should go to the other extreme and do nothing or even welcome a deterioration of the situation. We do not have the right to decide, for example, that people should be left to starve in order to increase their political awareness. Whether or not it would do so is beside the point; only the people who would actually do the starving have the right to make such a decision. But it is not necessarily better to do *anything* rather than to do nothing. Every action which we engage in, or which we dissuade others from engaging in, must be related to a critical analysis of the whole situation; and only socialism can provide such an analysis and the method of relating it to practice in a political praxis. While there is a need for a multiple strategy in order to bring about change, there is no room for conflicting ones.

There is no conflict, from the point of view of a White Christian, among the three major, positive forces for change in South Africa: Black Consciousness, Christianity, and Socialism. None, from this same perspective, provides a total world view by answering all man's needs in its own esoteric way. Black Consciousness articulates the rejection by the oppressed of their present condition and of any White-imposed alternative. This presents a challenge both to the present political system and to the distorted Christianity which has served as a legitimisation of it. Christianity demands a rejection of the same system and, more specifically, a response to the Black rejection of it. Socialism provides the only effective method of doing this. There is no question of substituting socialism for Christianity; socialism is the indispensable means of giving practical effect to a Christian concern for one's neighbour. How Blacks and/or non-Christian socialists integrate these three forces is not my immediate concern, but I believe that a political praxis must integrate them, not only for that praxis to be morally acceptable to Christians, but also for it to be politically effective and to lead to the creation of a truly human society in this particular historical and social context.

The radical change which is demanded by Christianity and which is given political expression in socialism is in fact in the interests of Whites as well as of Blacks. But it is in their human interests rather than in their short term economic interests, and it is unlikely that many Whites will sacrifice the latter in favour of the former. It is more important, however, for the interest of South Africa as a whole, that a few Whites wholeheartedly accept the need for, and work towards, radical change than that the White population as a whole be prepared to make some 'concessions'. When Blacks finally attain power, it is hardly likely that they are going to differentiate between Whites who call them 'kaffirs' and those who call them 'Bantu'.

In the meantime, bridges cannot be built between oppressors and oppressed. Bridges cannot be built at multiracial, 'liberal' tea parties because the lack of such parties is not the reason for people actually being hungry. For as long as 'White interests' means the freedom to exploit others there can be nothing but polarisation between the races, because 'others' means Blacks. The time for building bridges is when people are no longer divided into oppressed and oppressors, exploiters and exploited. The immediate task is to oppose, not to disguise or smooth over, all forms of oppression and exploitation. Those who are engaged in this task now will be the only ones in a position to build the bridges when the time comes.

To persist with a 'liberal' political approach serves only to perpetuate the false consciousness which blinds both oppressed and oppressor to the true nature of their condition. By exposing and attacking the root cause of the evils of our society one helps to dispel this false consciousness. It is the task of Blacks to overcome the false racial consciousness among Blacks, but Whites have a part to play in overcoming the false political, economic and religious consciousness.

This is not a purely intellectual exercise. For, as Freire says, 'if those who were once naive continue their new apprenticeship, they will come to understand that consciousness is not changed by lessons, lectures and eloquent sermons but by the actions of human beings on the world' (*op. cit.,* p. 102). The precise form that these actions will take will be determined in the course of the apprenticeship. They cannot be planned in advance.

As Christians, we believe that the ultimate resolution of the conflict between good and evil lies in the triumph of the good; not in a compromise between the two. Even though the immediate prospects for radical change appear dim we must not come to terms with the present system. Our fulfilment, satisfaction and salvation must be found in our efforts - most probably our failures - to bring about radical change, not in the prospect or achievement of success. The roughest part of the road to success still has to be travelled.

'Moderate' White political 'opposition' groups will be allowed to continue playing their games and pleading with the Nationalists to introduce changes. Not only are the Nationalists not threatened by such pleadings, they can even afford to welcome them. But they will not tolerate *any* opposition which seeks to expose and overcome the root cause of oppression and which thus threatens their hold on power. It would be foolhardy to *seek* a direct confrontation with the power that the Nationalists command, but we can hardly avoid it. 'If we are sowing something really new, it is inevitable that the community of faith and the existing order are on a collision course. Persecution will come. It is time to stop planting pumpkins. Let us plant dates, even though those who plant them will never eat them. If our child was aborted, let us lay eggs which will be hatched long after we are dead.' (Alves, *op.cit.*, p. 204).

I would not like to make a definite prediction about how long the incubation period will be in South Africa, but I think it will be a very long time before we have a free and politically integrated society which acknowledges cultural and religious differences. But we will never have it if we continue to be concerned with 'souls' rather than human beings, and if we are more interested in things than in people.

Bibliography

Abbott, W.M. (ed.) *The Documents of Vatican II* (London and Dublin, 1966)

Alves, R.A. *Tomorrow's Child: Imagination, Creativity and the Rebirth of Culture* (New York, 1972)

Assman, H. *Practical Theology of Liberation* (London, 1975)

Bonhoeffer, D. *Letters and Papers from Prison* (London and Glasgow, 1959)

Bonino, J.M. *Doing Theology in a Revolutionary Situation* (Philadelphia, 1975)

— *Christians and Marxists* (London, 1976)

Davies, J.D. *Beginning Now* (London, 1971)

— *Good News in Galatians* (Glasgow, 1975)

Davies, J.G. *Christians, Politics and Violent Revolution* (London, 1976)

de Rosa, P. *Christ and Original Sin* (London, 1967)

Dewart, L. *The Future of Belief: Theism in a World Come of Age* (London, 1967)

Durrwell, F.X. *The Resurrection: A Biblical Study* (London and New York, 1960)

Fransen, P. *Intelligent Theology*, vol. I and vol. III (London, 1969)

Freire, P. *Education for Critical Consciousness* (London, 1974)

Gollwitzer, H. *The Christian Faith and The Marxist Criticism of Religion* (Edinburgh, 1970)

Gonzales-Ruiz, J.M. *The New Creation: Marxist and Christian?* (New York, 1976)

Griffiths, B. (ed.) *Is Revolution Change?* (London, 1972)

Gutierrez, G. *A Theology of Liberation* (London, 1974)

Johnstone, F.A. *Class, Race and Gold* (London, 1976)

Kee, A. (ed.) *A Reader in Political Theology* (London, 1974)

Machovec, M. *A Marxist Looks at Jesus* (London, 1976)

Middleton, N. *The Language of Christian Revolution* (London and Sydney, 1968)

Miranda, J.P. *Marx and the Bible: A Critique of the Philosophy of Oppression* (London, 1977)

Nolan, A. *Jesus Before Christianity* (Cape Town, 1976)
Pannenberg, W. *Theology and the Kingdom of God* (Philadelphia, 1969)
Piediscalzi, N. and Thobaben, R.G. (eds) *From Hope to Liberation* (Philadelphia, 1974)
Ramsey, P. *Basic Christian Ethics* (New York, 1956)
Schillebeeckx, E. *God and Man* (London, 1969)
– *God the Future of Man* (London, 1969)
– *World and Church* (London and Sydney, 1971)
– *The Understanding of Faith* (London, 1974)
Segundo, J.L. *The Liberation of Theology* (Dublin, 1977)
Senghor, L.S. *On African Socialism* (London and Dunmow, 1964)
Simpson, M. *Death or Eternal Life* (Cork, 1970)
Sodepax Report, *In Search of a Theology of Development* (Geneva, 1969)
Stott, J.R.W. *Basic Christianity* (London, 1958)
Turner, R. *The Eye of the Needle* (Johannesburg, 1972)
Wright, H.N. *The Burden of the Present* (Cape Town, 1977)

Newspapers and journals
Daily News, Durban
Financial Mail, Johannesburg
New Blackfriars, Oxford
Rand Daily Mail, Johannesburg
South African Labour Bulletin, Durban
South African Outlook, Cape Town
Southern Cross, Cape Town
Sunday Tribune, Durban